leatherwork

craft **workshop**

leatherwork

25 practical ideas for hand-crafted leather projects that are easy to make at home

Mary Maguire

photography by Peter Williams

southwater

This edition is published by Southwater

Southwater is an imprint of Anness Publishing Ltd
Hermes House, 88–89 Blackfriars Road,
London SE1 8HA
tel. 020 7401 2077; fax 020 7633 9499
www.southwaterbooks.com; info@anness.com

© Anness Publishing Ltd 2000, 2004

UK agent: The Manning Partnership Ltd, 6 The Old
Dairy, Melcombe Road, Bath BA2 3LR;
tel. 01225 478444; fax 01225 478440;
sales@manning-partnership.co.uk

UK distributor: Grantham Book Services Ltd, Isaac
Newton Way, Alma Park Industrial Estate, Grantham,
Lincs NG31 9SD;
tel. 01476 541080; fax 01476 541061;
orders@gbs.tbs-ltd.co.uk

North American agent/distributor: National Book
Network, 4501 Forbes Boulevard, Suite 200, Lanham,
MD 20706;
tel. 301 459 3366; fax 301 429 5746;
www.nbnbooks.com

Australian agent/distributor: Pan Macmillan Australia,
Level 18, St Martins Tower, 31 Market St,
Sydney, NSW 2000;
tel. 1300 135 113; fax 1300 135 103;
customer.service@macmillan.com.au

New Zealand agent/distributor: David Bateman Ltd,
30 Tarndale Grove, Off Bush Road, Albany, Auckland;
tel. (09) 415 7664; fax (09) 415 8892

Publisher: Joanna Lorenz
Project Editor: Sarah Ainley
Copy Editor: Heather Dewhurst
Designer: Lilian Lindblom
Photographer: Peter Williams
Stylist: Georgina Rhodes
Illustrators: Madeleine David and Robert
Highton

Previously published as *New Crafts:
Leatherworks*

10 9 8 7 6 5 4 3 2 1

CONTENTS

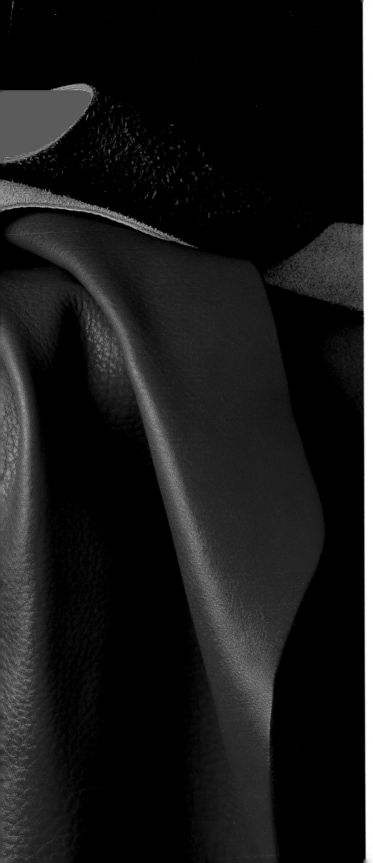

INTRODUCTION

LEATHER IS AN EXTRAORDINARILY BEAUTIFUL MATERIAL, AND ONE WHICH OFFERS GREAT POTENTIAL BECAUSE OF ITS VERSATILITY. HANDWORKING LEATHER IS AN AGE-OLD CRAFT, PRACTISED WORLDWIDE, AND THE TECHNIQUES USED TODAY FOR TANNING, DYEING AND SHAPING LEATHER ARE NOT DRAMATICALLY DIFFERENT FROM THOSE USED IN ANCIENT EGYPT HUNDREDS OF YEARS AGO. MODERN PRODUCTION METHODS MEAN THAT HIDES AND SKINS ARE NOW AVAILABLE IN A MULTITUDE OF COLOURS, WEIGHTS AND FINISHES, AND THIS OPENS UP POSSIBILITIES FOR WHAT CAN BE ACHIEVED. CLOTHING, ACCESSORIES AND SOFT FURNISHINGS CAN ALL BE PERSONALIZED WITH A CONTEMPORARY TWIST, AND THERE IS LIMITLESS OPPORTUNITY FOR SCULPTURE, JEWELLERY AND FURNITURE.

THIS BOOK IS DESIGNED FOR ALL LEVELS OF LEATHERWORKER. FOR THOSE STARTING OUT, THERE ARE DETAILED INSTRUCTIONS TO TEACH THE ESSENTIAL TECHNIQUES, AND THESE CAN BE DEVELOPED BY WORKING THROUGH THE 25 COMMISSIONED PROJECTS. NOVICE AND EXPERIENCED LEATHERWORKERS ALIKE CAN TAKE INSPIRATION FROM THE STUNNING COLLECTION OF INTERNATIONAL WORK FEATURED IN THE GALLERY SECTION, WHICH, IT IS HOPED, WILL PROVIDE A CREATIVE CHALLENGE AND ENCOURAGE FUTURE IDEAS FOR BEAUTIFULLY CRAFTED LEATHER PIECES.

Left: Colour, weight and texture all contribute to the beauty of leather. The simplest of leather projects can look fabulously stylish if put together with thought and care.

A History of Leather Work

ANIMAL SKINS ARE PROBABLY OUR EARLIEST FORM OF CLOTHING. AROUND 500,000 YEARS AGO OUR PRIMITIVE ANCESTORS SKINNED THE ANIMALS THEY ATE AND SCRAPED THE SKINS CLEAN TO WRAP AROUND THEMSELVES FOR WARMTH. BUT IT WAS NOT UNTIL TANNING WAS DISCOVERED THAT WE HAD LEATHER, A HARDWEARING PRESERVED MATERIAL, AND ONE OF OUR FIRST MANUFACTURED PRODUCTS. SINCE THEN, THE IMPORTANCE OF LEATHER HAS BEEN IMMEASURABLE.

Leather has been produced all over the world since ancient times, and tools of the trade survive from pre-dynastic Egypt. By dynastic times the Egyptians were making sophisticated leather goods – bags, cushion covers, flooring, harnesses, tyres (tires), shoes, sandals, dog collars, chair seats and tents. Leather was valued on a level with gold and silver and was considered a gift fit for kings and gods; many examples of Egyptian leatherware have been found preserved in the tombs of the Pharaohs.

In ancient Arabia at this time, tanning was a familiar process. Skins were treated using the pulverized stalks of the native chulga plant mixed with water. The Arabians developed elaborate leathercraft skills, particularly for saddlery, which was often bejewelled and highly ornate. This art was later passed to the Spanish via merchant trading with the Moors, and it came to South America with colonization of the New World in the 17th century.

The Hebrews are thought to have been the first to use oak bark tanning, and their methods are still in use today. Traditionally, the hides were packed into a pit in the ground and then soaked in a pickle made from ground oak bark, berries and roots, for several months. They would then be stretched out, smoothed flat and left to dry in the open air. Other treatments still in use include "shamoying", referred to in Homer's epic poem, *The Iliad*.

Right: Accessories made by Northern Plains Native Americans in the second half of the 19th century: (from right) beaded skin case and pipe bag; papoose carrier; knife sheath; artist's ornate bag, pouch, emblem and slippers.

Native Americans also produced the soft and pliable buckskin tan, which had the added bonus of being water resistant.

The benefits of leather as a hardwearing material were quickly recognized, and leather has been used for armoury since records began. Leather-covered wooden shields were used worldwide, and the armies of ancient Greece wore boots, shirts, leg guards and helmets, all made from leather. Anglo-Saxon soldiers wore leather pantaloons strengthened with steel mesh, with leather cone-shaped skull caps on their heads. The Roman army invaded Britain wearing leather hats and sandals; while in China, leather scales were linked together as armour in the 3rd century.

Left: Sturdy leather was the practical choice for protective headgear. This example shows a fireman's helmet worn in the Great Fire of London in the 16th century.

Below: A pair of gentlewoman's gloves of white kid leather, embroidered with silver thread and sequins.

This technique softens the hide to produce a leather known as shamoy or chamois. It involves washing the hide repeatedly, stretching it out on a wooden frame, rubbing oil into the pores and beating it. Another common practice in ancient Greece was to build tanneries outside city walls, spreading the wet skins out on the walkways to be softened by the passing feet of citizens. A mixture of wine and water was used by the Greeks, Romans and Egyptians for dehairing skins.

Native Americans had been producing leather for hundreds of years before the Europeans reached America, using it to make clothing, tents and canoes. The Crow Indians are said to have had the best tanning methods (the skins were immersed in an ash solution, then cleaned and smoked), while the Navajo were known for their beautifully dressed, decorative hides.

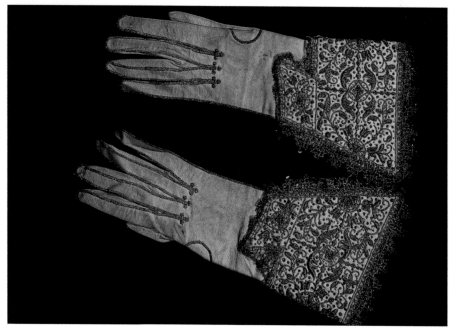

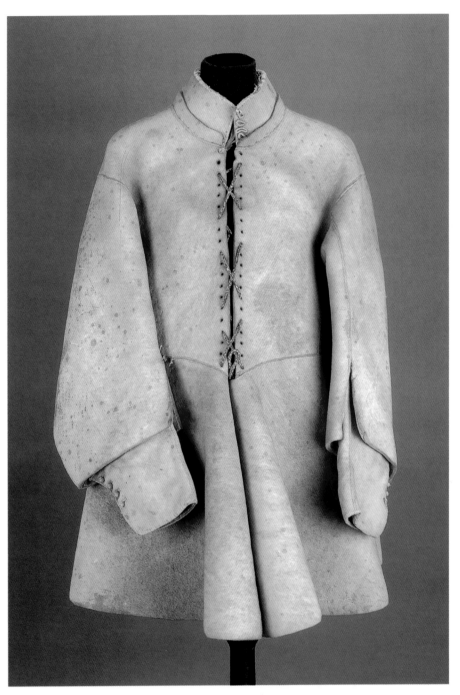

Above: A buff coat of soft grey leather with front lacing and buttoned inner cuffs. The coat is dated c.1643, and is typical of a light summer coat worn by men in the 17th century.

During the 13th century, the explorer Marco Polo wrote that the war tents of the Kublai Khan were made of lion skins joined so finely that neither wind nor rain could penetrate. His soldiers were dressed in buffalo hide, as were the four elephants that carried his wooden castle to battle. He also noted that when he visited India he saw soft, delicate bed coverlets made of red and blue leather and stitched with silver and gold thread. India has long been renowned for its fine decorative leather-work, especially that of slippers.

In Russia and Poland, leather was used as a form of money, first as a roughly cut rectangle, which evolved into a circular piece and was later embossed with its value. Leather currency remained in general circulation up until the time of Peter the Great in the 17th century.

Britain has had a long history of leather tanning. A leather cup found preserved in mud in Smithfields, London, in 1867 is believed to have been made in neolithic times. By the 11th century, a wide variety of goods was being produced, as recorded by one Saxon writer. Britain was perfectly suited to producing leather: herds of cattle had been domesticated since primitive times and the countryside had a plentiful supply of oak trees rich in tannic acid.

By the Middle Ages, leatherworkers had organized themselves into one of the earliest and most influential guilds, the Guild of the Saddlers and Skinners. A similar workers' guild, the Fraternity of Leatherworkers, was operating in France and was controlled by the Church.

Workers' guilds were very powerful organizations. They had strict rules, and would punish bad workmanship and destroy faulty work to ensure quality craftsmanship. To protect the standard of work, goods could only be sold in daylight hours when the work could be inspected.

Each trade area needed its own guild to maintain standards and others were soon formed, such as the Pursers, Girdlers, Tanners, and Cordwainers.

The word "cordwainer" was derived from Cordovan, an area of Spain that produced cordwain, a soft leather made from horse, goat and kid hides. The leather was tanned by a method developed by the Moors, using allum and salt. Being white in colour, cordwain leather could be dyed in brilliant shades and decorated with gold and silver. It was used for wall hangings and upholstery, and was ideal for making the fashionably long, pointed-toe shoes, which were popular with men and women in medieval times.

Leather permeated every aspect of medieval life: leather doublet and hose were the dress of the times; travel was dependent on leather for harnesses and saddles, for the leather-covered framework of the coaches they pulled, and for the leather trunks and cases used to carry goods; money was kept in leather pouches; drink was poured from leather jugs and drunk from leather vessels; there were even leather lanterns. Every trade needed leather adapted to its function – soft and stretchy for gloves, or thick and strong for shoe soles – and tanners began to specialize.

During the Industrial Revolution in the 18th century, leather was used, amongst other things, to make the belts to drive the machines in the factories, to line the rollers, and to furnish the interiors of trains. Leather was being tanned in much the same way as of old, until an Englishman, Sir Humphrey Davy (the inventor of the miner's lamp), experimented with tanning and found that by using chestnut wood, quebracho (a South American tree), hemlock bark and myrabalams (an Indian fruit), he could produce different kinds of vegetable-tanned leather.

Chrome-tanned leather came later, when an American chemist, Augustus Schultz, discovered that chromium salts could make leather water resistant. Early results were blue in colour, and the leather had to be softened with soap and oil. Today, chrome-tanned leather comes in a range of colours and is the most suitable material for footwear, although shoe soles are still made of vegetable-tanned leather.

With the development of man-made materials came a sharp decline in the need for handcrafted leather. But as an art form leather offers enormous potential, and today's artists take inspiration from both traditional and modern influences to create their own new and exciting work.

Above: A 16th-century young man's jerkin of brown leather. The peascod belly and wings are quilted with metal thread in padded ribs, and are slashed to reveal rich burgundy velvet.

GALLERY

LEATHER IS A HIGHLY POPULAR MATERIAL AMONG ARTISTS AND CRAFTSPEOPLE BECAUSE OF ITS STRENGTH, THE EASE WITH WHICH IT CAN BE MOULDED AND SHAPED, AND ITS NATURAL BEAUTY. DRAWING ON INFLUENCES ANCIENT AND MODERN, PRACTICAL AND INSPIRED, THE INTERNATIONAL COLLECTION OF ARTISTS BROUGHT TOGETHER HERE ALL SHOW INGENUITY AND SKILL IN INTERPRETATION AND TECHNIQUE, AND THE RESULT IS A WONDERFULLY DIVERSE RANGE OF STYLES.

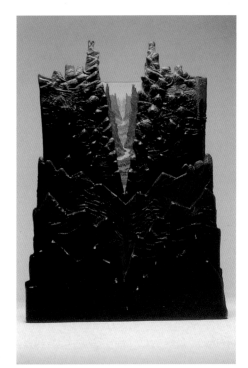

Above: NEW DIRECTIONS IN BOOKBINDING AND THE BOOK: ART & OBJECT
This piece makes up part of a collection to explore the possibilities of bookbinding. It plays with a fantasy theme and the idea of the book as a magical journey, with ever-winding glimpses of soft green pasture to invite the reader in. The heavily tooled leather provides visual impact with its multi-dimensional texture. PHILIP SMITH

Right: WESTERN SADDLE
This award-winning saddle is a example of classic leatherwork. Traditionally, the Western saddle offers greater potential for decoration than the English saddle, and the stirrup leathers here have been thonged as embellishment. Photographed by Peter Williams.
PETER NORRINGTON

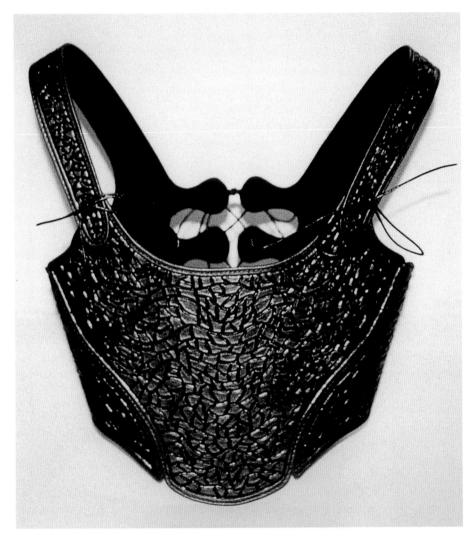

Left: CROPPED CORSET
Vegetable-tanned tooling leather has been used to create this textured corset. The pattern was cut freehand from leather, using a swivel knife. The cut lines were then opened with narrow spoon modelling, and the bevelled effect was created using a ball modelling tool. The corset has been hand-painted using ceramic and antique dyes in bronze and black.
PAUL SEVILLE

Below: DRAGON HORN, 1993
This decorative hunting horn explores the acoustic properties of leather. The leather has been sculptured into a perfect horn, which adds the dimension of sound to the visual idea of the dragon head and scales. Photographed by Peter Clark.
GARRY GREENWOOD

Right: "BUCKET", 1997
This sleek and deceptively simple handbag has been designed to enhance the beauty of the materials used to make it. The cool aluminium handle contrasts visually with the leather, and adds a tactile quality to the bag.
STEVEN HARKIN

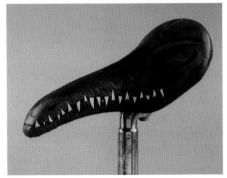

Left: BICYCLE SADDLE, "CROCO"
This crocodile face, complete with fearsome teeth, adds an imaginative touch to an otherwise functional feature of bicycle design. The croc's face has been hand-painted on to vegetable-tanned leather, stretched into place over the saddle.
STEPHANIE ROTHEMUND

Right: BOWL
Cuir bouilli (boiled leather) cow hide has been sculptured into shape to create this impressive bowl. Heat-hardening the hide in this way has enabled the artist to produce a functional stand-alone structure.
REX LINGWOOD

Below: HOLSTER
Oak-tanned leather has been shaped and intricately carved to form this beautiful pistol holster. Photographed by Peter Williams.
PETER NORRINGTON

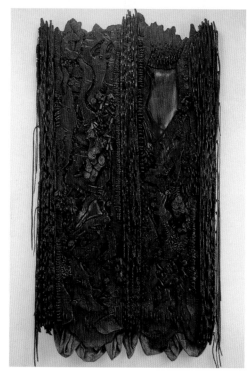

Above: MOULDED PURSE ON BELT
Oak-tanned cow hide has been used as the basis for this stylish accessory. The purse and belt are both lined with soft and malleable pig skin.
VALERIE MICHAEL

Left: "TEXTURA"
This intriguing piece was designed as a mystical garden-of-the-mind and an invitation to personal reflection. The tooled leather takes on the appearance of varnished wood, and the deep colour tone and heavy texture form their own visual harmony.
JOSÉ BERNARDO

Left: (From left)
"MINOTAUR MASK
BOX", "AZTEC WEST",
"PROMETHEUS"
Mythology has dictated
form for each of these
sculptured, coloured and
polished leather boxes.
(Patrick Shanahan/
Crafts Council)
TIM MEAGHER

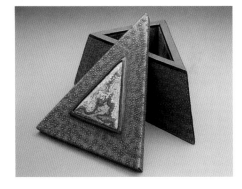

Left: LAMINATED
BOWL: "BIRD"
The Japanese tradition
of "Urishi", which involves
the use of protective
laquer and modern resin
materials on leather, has
given a highly polished
appearance to this leather
bowl in an exploration of
the artist's fascination with
beauty and usefulness.
JUN NAKAHAMA

Above: TEXTURED
ANGLES
The semi-precious stone
incorporated in the design
of this sculptured box was
the influence for the form
and colour of the finished
piece. The box is both
functional and ornate,
and it represents a
celebration of man's
use of natural materials.
TODD BARBER

MATERIALS

FOR A FULL RANGE OF LEATHER HIDES AND SKINS, VISIT YOUR LOCAL TANNERY OR CONTACT ONE OF THE WHOLESALE SUPPLIERS LISTED AT THE BACK OF THE BOOK. LARGER DEPARTMENT STORES USUALLY STOCK PRE-DYED LEATHER. VISIT FLEA MARKETS AND SECOND-HAND STORES FOR CLOTHING AND ACCESSORIES.

Lambskin derives from the natural casualties of the lambing season, when four per cent of lambs are stillborn. Because the skins are from the newborn lambs, they are soft enough to be stitched by hand. Lambskin comes in a range of colours, and looks and feels delightful. The skins are inexpensive and small.

Suede clothing can be used to make economical suede leather projects. Second-hand suede clothing is inexpensive to buy, and is easy to find in charity (thrift) shops and flea markets.

Chamois leather is a wonderfully soft, machine washable leather. Chamois leather is used for window cleaning, which means it is widely available and cheap to buy.

Leather stain can be either water- or spirit- (alcohol-) based. The stains used in this book are water-based and are used to colour natural leather. The stain penetrates into the leather, unlike acrylic dyes, which lie on the surface in the same way as paint.

Leather finishing, dressing or polish are needed to feed and polish dyed and natural leathers. If the leather has been bought pre-dyed, it will usually have been treated with a finish.

Thonging is available in suede or leather in a wide colour range. When making a lacing pattern, choose thonging with a semi-round profile to help it slip more easily through the plaiting (braiding).

Interfacing is useful for backing leather that is too flimsy to hold its form.

Velcro tape is used to make quick-fastening tabs and straps, and is widely available from craft stores. Stitch the tape in place wherever needed.

Sinew or cord is a thin leather cord which is used as lacing or embellishment.

Linen thread, available in thick or fine widths, is used for most kinds of leather-work. The thread is strong and hardwearing, and is used in combination with beeswax, which strengthens and water-proofs it, and helps it to slip more easily through the leather.

Felt-tipped pens, both translucent and opaque, are useful materials to keep in stock. Translucent pens allow the grain of the leather to show through the colour, while the opaque colour lies on the surface. Treat pen-coloured leather with beeswax before polishing it.

Eyelet holes are used to reinforce holes punched for lacing in shoes, clothing and accessories. Eyelet holes are now available in different sizes and finishes, including silver, gilt, copper or antiqued effect. Use eyelet holes with a two-part eyelet kit.

Rivets are designed to join two or more materials together. They are available in different width cap sizes and in three lengths of shank, and it is useful to keep as varied a supply as possible in stock. Use rivets with a rivet setter.

Cowhide strips are bought pre-dyed or in the natural undyed form, as preferred. Use cowhide strips for making narrow-width accessories such as belts, guitar straps, luggage straps and bag handles.

Embroidery cotton (floss), available from general craft suppliers, is used to add fine details and decoration to leather projects. Wax the cotton before stitching it through leather to strengthen it and make it waterproof.

Leather hide is bought by the full skin or in sections: belly, back, side, bend or double shoulder, or by the square foot (30 x 30 cm). Buy direct from a tannery for an economical price. The weight of the leather is an indication of its thickness.

Pig skin is a soft, supple leather which is characterized by its distinctive grain (the hairs grow in groups of three on a pig).

Deer skin is specially tanned to be soft and flexible.

Metallic finished leather is coloured in a variety of metallic colours, including gold and silver.

Skiving leather is a natural undyed hide which has been skived (pared down) to make it thin enough for moulding.

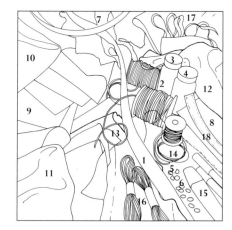

KEY

1 Leather strapping	8 Interfacing	14 Linen thread
2 Suede thonging	9 Vegetable-tanned	15 Felt-tipped pens
3 Wax	leather	16 Embroidery
4 Water-soluble dye	10 Deer skin	cotton (floss)
5 Rivets	11 Pig skin	17 Suede clothing
6 Eyelet holes	12 Chamois leather	18 Velcro tape
7 Lambskin	13 Leather thonging	

EQUIPMENT

LEATHERWORKING TOOLS ARE SATISFYING TO USE, AND PROVIDING THEY ARE WELL LOOKED AFTER, THEY SHOULD LAST FOR MANY YEARS. BUY THE MORE SPECIALIST TOOLS AS YOU NEED THEM, AND BUILD YOUR COLLECTION AS YOU DEVELOP YOUR SKILLS. QUALITY TOOLS USUALLY MAKE A BETTER INVESTMENT.

Latex gloves offer protection for the hands when using dyes or finishes.

Sponge and water are used to dampen or shape leather, or to apply dyes.

Clam(p)s are essential for hand-stitching. The clam(also known as clamp) grips the leather and is held between the knees.

Stitching ponies are used with clamps and are designed to project upwards from between the knees, leaving the hands free for stitching.

Bone folders are polished pieces of bone. They are useful for smoothing creases, burnishing edges, folding and slicking.

Stitching or sewing palms protect the fingers when stitching.

Fids are blunt awls which are useful for enlarging holes in leather in order to insert lacing. Fids can also be used to tighten or loosen leather knots.

Awls are extremely useful tools for piercing and stitching leather.

Rulers, both metal and plastic, are used to take measurements. Use strong, metal rulers when marking and cutting leather with a craft knife.

Glovers needles have a three-sided point which acts as a cutting edge. They are available from specialist suppliers in sizes ranging from 000 to No 7.

Leather needles are more sturdy than embroidery needles, which makes them ideal for sewing through leather.

Slot punches are used to punch slots into straps or belts when adding buckles.

Riveting domes have a concave head to protect the rivet when hammering.

Eyelet punches are the two-part kits used for setting eyelet holes in leather.

Rotary leather punches are used to make holes in leather. Choose a quality punch with replaceable cutting tubes.

Edge slickers are run along the edge of moistened leather for a smooth finish.

Cutting mats will protect your work surface when working with a craft knife.

Beeswax allows stitching thread to slip through holes. It also makes it waterproof.

Epoxy glue is a strong two-part glue which gives a very secure join.

PVA (white) glue is a general-purpose glue for joining lighter pieces of leather.

Leather hammers have round, polished faces to protect leather when hammering.

Riveting hammers are used with rivets. Ordinary hammers can also be used.

Hide mallets are designed to prevent scarring to the hide when hammering.

Pegs, clips and clamps are used to hold leather in place when gluing or shaping.

Blocks of end grain should be used when punching and chiseling to protect tools from blunting.

Pieces of wood will help to protect the work surface when riveting leather.

Paintbrushes are useful for applying paints, dressings and PVA (white) glue.

Thonging/lacing needles are made from tempered spring steel. The needle head is split into two prongs and the lacing is held between clips in the prongs.

Craft knives are useful for cutting leather.

Stitching wheels mark out stitching positions on leather. The number of teeth on the wheel determines the stitch size.

Adjustable stitch groovers are run along the edge of the leather to cut narrow, parallel grooves to use as a stitching guide.

Edge bevellers are used to trim and neaten the edges of leather.

Skivers are used to skive (pare down) leather without cutting too deep.

Scissors are used for general cutting.

Leather scissors are blunt-pointed and sturdy and will cut leather well.

Pinking shears are used to add decorative edging to lightweight leathers.

Stitching chisels are used to punch holes at regular intervals.

Single stitching chisels are used where multiple holes would be inappropriate, for example around curved corners.

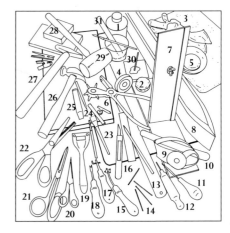

KEY

1 Contact adhesive	11 Thonging awl	22 Pinking shears
2 Beeswax	12 Awl	23 Pronged skiver
3 Latex gloves	13 Metal rulers	24 Rivet setter
4 Edge slicker	14 Leather needles	25 Slot punch
5 Sponge	15 Stitching wheel	26 Leatherworkers'
6 Rotary leather	16 Craft knife	hammer
punch	17 Stitch groover	27 Riveting hammer
7 Stitching pony	18 Edge beveller	28 Block of end grain
8 Stitching clam(p)	19 Skiver	29 Hide mallet
9 Stitchng palm	20 Embroidery scissors	30 Epoxy glue
10 Bone folder	21 Leather scissors	31 PVA (white) glue

BASIC TECHNIQUES

Aknowledge of the essential leatherworking techniques will allow you to make the projects in this book. It is a good idea to practise on scraps of leather until you are comfortable with the techniques. Refer back to these pages, if necessary, as you work through the projects.

PUNCHING

USING A SLOT PUNCH

1 When punching with a rotary punch it is best to place a scrap piece of thick leather underneath the item that you are punching. This protects the ends of the cutting tubes from blunting against the metal. If you need to get to a point beyond the reach of the punch, try folding over the leather and inserting it, or gathering it up into the jaws of the punch.

2 When the part of the leather you are trying to punch is inaccessible to a rotary punch and you do not have a single punch, place the item to be punched on a wooden board with a thick piece of scrap leather beneath the spot to be punched, and another thick piece of leather between the jaws of the punch. Close the punch tightly and hit the bottom (which will be facing upwards) with a hide mallet.

Punches come in many shapes and sizes, some purely decorative and some strictly functional. Good punches designed for cutting smartly through leather are made from carbon steel with hardened cutting edges. They are expensive and it is important to use them correctly. Always lay the article being punched on either a block of end grain of wood or a special cutting pad. This will prevent damage to the work surface and will limit wear of the punch. A slot punch is a worthwhile investment for your tool box. It is designed to fit the centre bow of a buckle, allowing the prong to project through.

SKIVING

Skiving or paring leather is like planing wood, only you pull the skiving tool towards you and it shaves off thin slithers of leather. Use it on any place where the leather needs to be pared down, such as on belts where the leather doubles over to hold the buckle. Without skiving it would be too bulky. Skive it so that it gradually reduces in thickness rather than jumping from one thickness to another. Hold the leather very securely while you pull the tool towards you. The more pressure you put on the tool, the deeper the cut will be.

EDGE BEVELLING

Use this technique to form a graduated or rounded edge. It is a smooth way to finish belts, and will take the square off the belt edge. Edge bevellers are available in different widths. To use one, hold the belt securely while you apply even pressure along the edge of a strip of leather. Make sure your fingers are not in the firing line in case you slip.

EDGE SLICKING

Once the edges have been bevelled, they often appear coarse or fibrous. By slicking the edge you compact the fibres into a smooth rounded surface. First damp the edge with a moist sponge or cloth. Then rub the slicker backwards and forwards over a small area at a time.

RIVETING

Riveting is a quick and easy way of securing two or more surfaces together. One makes a very strong join (seam) and saves doing lots of stitching. Rivets come in different width sizes and lengths and are available in different finishes, such as gilt, brass, antiqued nickel and copper. The projects in this book use medium and long nickle rivets.

Rivets have two components, a shank and a cap. Before riveting, you must punch appropriate-sized holes in the leather to be joined. Line up the holes and insert the shank through the hole on the underside of the leather (the side of the finished product that will not be seen). Press the domed cap on to the shank and place the rivet setter (a cylindrical implement with a concave end that fits over the cap of the rivet) over the rivet. A riveting hammer or an ordinary hammer can be used to knock the rivet into place.

MOULDING LEATHER

Vegetable-tanned, undyed leather has the ability, once dampened, to be moulded into all sorts of shapes and to retain those shapes once dry. Throughout history this technique has been used to produce shields, drinking vessels, helmets and sculptures. Once this type of leather is soaked in water, its fibres become soft and pliable and it is easy to shape or emboss. It can be formed into shapes with the use of moulds or freely by hand. It helps to have warm water and gentle heat. But for the basic moulding project shown in this book, the leather does not need soaking, just dampening with a sponge. When damp, press into the desired shape.

DYEING LEATHER

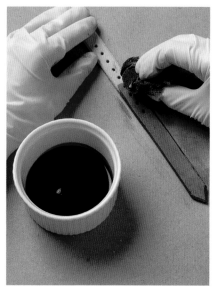

It is a good idea to test areas of scrap leather when trying a new dye. Protect your work surface and, if using spirit- (alcohol-) based dyes, work in a well-ventilated area.

The surface of the leather must be clean, as grease marks can resist the absorption of the dye. The surface of the leather can be washed to remove grease marks. This is not a process suitable to do with children as the mixture is poisonous. Wearing protective gloves, make a solution of oxalic acid (5 ml/1 tsp to 600 ml/ 1 pint water). Using a soft cloth, gently rub the surface of the leather, then let dry.

To apply the dye, first dampen the leather with a piece of sponge or cotton wool (cotton ball). Apply the dye with a soft cloth, beginning in one corner of the leather and working in a circular motion over the surface. It is easier to obtain an even colour if you apply several layers.

FINISHING

Natural leather that has been dyed needs to be dressed with a polish or a finish to make the colour permanent. The dressing feeds and seals the surface of the leather, preventing it from drying out, and protecting water-based dyes from running.

THONGING

Double Loop

1 Mark a line, dampen with a sponge and run the stitch marker along. Using this as a guide, punch holes for the thong.

2 Working from the front using a flat thonging needle, pass the thong through the first hole, leaving an end as shown, and over the top and back through the second hole. Now pass the needle between the cross of the thong from the bottom to the top.

3 Keep working in this way along the stitch line: through a hole, back over and through the cross, which is one stitch back. Make sure the good side of the thong is showing on the surface.

4 At the corner, go through each of the three corner holes twice to make the woven pattern work around the corner. Cut the 90-degree corner off the leather: it is easier to pass the thong around two 45-degree corners.

Triple Loop

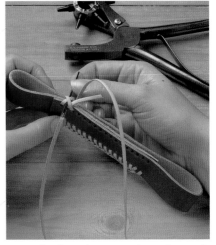

1 Mark a line, dampen and run the stitch marker over before punching the holes. Start at the second hole and pass the needle through the first hole to form the cross of thonging, then go through the third hole.

2 Continue to pass the needle along the leather in this way, moving forward to the next hole and passing back to the hole before, to form the cross of thonging.

STITCHING TECHNIQUES

Preparing a Thread

1 Lay the thread end on a bench or block of wood. Place the blade of a knife on the thread, angled at 45 degrees away from you. Draw the thread towards you, applying a little pressure; the thread will unravel. Keep working until the threads have a silk-like quality. Work a few strokes at the tip to taper the end of the thread.

2 Wax the thread by rubbing it several times across a block of beeswax until it is well coated. Work the wax well into the tip using your fingers.

3 Pull the thread 5 cm (2 in) through the eye of the needle and then spike it with the end of the needle. Draw this thread end back along the needle and pull towards the eye to lock the thread in place. Rub the thread with beeswax.

Back Stitch

1 Prepare the leather as before, but this time only stitch grooving one side. Prepare a thread with one needle. Pierce three holes and, working from the left, pass the thread through the second and back through the first and pull up tight, leaving a short end to be woven in on the left side. Pass the thread through the third hole, leaving a loop.

2 Pass the thread back through the second hole and under the loop, first pulling the left side of the loop and then the right. Pierce the next hole and continue along the leather in the same way.

Saddle Stitch

1 Prepare the stitch line with the stitch groover. The stitch line should be the same distance from the edge as the thickness of the leather. Repeat on all pieces of leather to be stitched.

2 Choose a suitably-sized stitching wheel and dampen the groove with a sponge. Then run the stitch marker along the line.

3 Prepare a thread and needle for each end, and place the leather in a stitching pony. Using a stitching awl, pierce a hole in the leather, working from the front, on the right-hand side. Take the thread evenly through the first hole and then pierce the second hole.

4 Thread the needle through the hole. Holding the two needles as shown will help you with the next step.

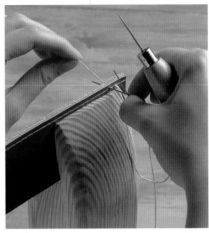

5 Next, put the right needle through the same hole, pulling the left thread back so that you do not spike it, and pull the needle through.

6 Holding the needles and thread as shown, pull the stitch up tight. The trick with saddle stitching is to hold both needles at the same time, although this may feel awkward at first.

SUEDE TASSELS

ELABORATE TASSELS ARE POPULAR IN INTERIOR DECORATION, THOUGH THEY CAN BE EXPENSIVE TO BUY. SUEDE OR LEATHER TASSELS ARE VERY EFFECTIVE AND HIGHLY INDIVIDUAL. THE TASSELS HERE ARE MADE FROM THICK SUEDE; THE THINNER THE MATERIAL THE SKINNIER THE TASSEL. THE PATTERN SIZE CAN BE ADAPTED FOR LARGER OR SMALLER TASSELS. TO ACHIEVE THE CURLY EFFECT AS SHOWN ON THE GREEN TASSEL, CUT THE SLOTS AT A JAUNTY ANGLE.

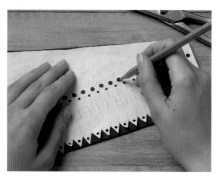

1 Make a paper stencil following the template at the back of the book. Place the stencil on the suede or leather and cut out the shape to form the basis of the tassel. Mark out all points to be punched with a pencil.

2 Cut out the triangular points with scissors. Punch out the large holes using a No 5 hole punch, and the smaller holes using No 1.

3 Using a metal ruler and craft knife, cut slits in the leather, following the markings on the template.

4 Carefully cut fringing in the leather from the inner points of the triangular edging up to each first small hole. Taking each pointed end of fringing in turn, loop it back and pull it through each respective slit to create a decorative twist.

5 Thread thick cord through the single hole in the corner of the shallower end of the suede. Tie a knot in the end of the cord and wrap your tassel base around it, starting from the wider edge.

6 Tie a knot at the end of a length of suede thonging. Thread through the hole in the top corner. Wrap it around the tassel three or four times and secure it by threading it through the last large hole on the bottom row. Knot and trim.

MATERIALS AND EQUIPMENT YOU WILL NEED
PAPER • PENCIL • SCISSORS • 15 x 23 CM (6 x 9 IN) SUEDE OR LEATHER • STRONG SCISSORS • HOLE PUNCH (NO 1 AND NO 5) • METAL RULER • CRAFT KNIFE • THICK CORD • SUEDE THONGING

BUNNY EGG COSIES

A SPECIAL PROJECT TO GRACE YOUR EASTER TABLE AND DELIGHT THE CHILDREN, THESE BUNNY EGG COSIES ARE MADE FROM LEFT-OVER SCRAPS OF LAMBSWOOL, SIMPLY STITCHED AROUND THE EDGE. THE INSERTION OF PIPE CLEANERS ALLOWS THE EARS TO STAY UPRIGHT OR BE BENT INTO DIFFERENT POSITIONS. BUTTONS HAVE BEEN USED FOR THE EYES, BUT YOU COULD STICK ON GOGGLY EYES, WHICH ARE AVAILABLE FROM GOOD CRAFT SUPPLIERS.

1 Cut out two bunny cosy shapes from lambskin following the templates at the back of the book. With woolly sides facing outwards, stitch the back and front pieces together along one side and over the ears. Then pause at the position shown, leaving the thread connected.

2 Insert a pipe cleaner along the seam of one ear and glue it in place. Fill the head with stuffing, pushing it in with a pencil. Insert a pipe cleaner into the other ear, and finish stitching the pieces together.

3 Using pink silk ribbon, stitch a cross stitch on the bunny's face for a nose. Secure with tiny stitches on the underside.

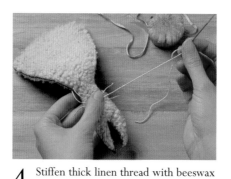

4 Stiffen thick linen thread with beeswax for the whiskers. Cut a length of thread and tie a knot 2 cm (¾ in) from the end. Push the needle and thread through the face from one cheek to the other. The thread will stop at the knot, creating the first whisker. Tie another knot up against the second cheek where the thread emerges and snip off the second whisker. Make another two pairs of whiskers.

5 Using a scrap of white lambskin, form a puff shape for the bunny's tail, adding a stitch to hold the shape.

6 Stitch the fluffy tail into position on the back of the bunny. Stitch on a small button for each of the bunny's eyes.

MATERIALS AND EQUIPMENT YOU WILL NEED

SCRAPS OF LAMBSKIN • PENCIL • SCISSORS • NEEDLE • LINEN THREAD • 2 PIPE CLEANERS • PVA (WHITE) GLUE • POLYESTER STUFFING • PINK SILK RIBBON • BEESWAX • SMALL BUTTONS OR GOGGLY EYES

COASTER AND NAPKIN RING

SIMPLICITY AND STYLE ARE COMBINED IN THIS EASY-TO-MAKE, USEFUL PROJECT SUITABLE FOR THE NOVICE LEATHERWORKER, WHETHER CHILD OR ADULT. SCRAP SUEDE CAN BE USED AS THE REQUIRED PIECES ARE ONLY SMALL. IF YOU WANT TO EXTEND THE THEME YOU COULD MAKE A SET WITH MATCHING PLACE MATS: THE SUBTLE DESIGN IS UNLIKELY TO OVERPOWER THE TABLESETTING. CHOOSE COLOURS SUITED TO YOUR TABLEWARE AND LINEN.

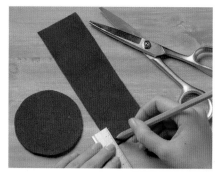

1 Cut a circle measuring 7 cm (2¾ in) in diameter and a strip measuring 18 x 6 cm (7 x 2½ in) from thick suede or leather. Mark out four holes at each end of the strip with a pencil. The outer holes should be 5 mm (¼ in) from the short edge and 1 cm (½ in) from the long edge. The inner holes should be parallel to these but 2 cm (¾ in) from the short edge.

2 Wrap the strip into a cylinder to line up the marked holes. Hold securely as you punch through the two layers.

3 Using leather thonging, stitch the ends of the strip together through the holes to make a cross. Tie the knots on the inside of the ring and trim to neaten.

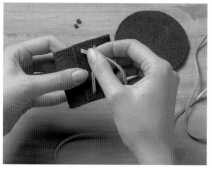

4 Mark a smaller circle on the coaster, 5 mm (¼ in) from the outer edge, and punch holes around this circle at regular intervals.

5 Using leather thonging, overstitch around the circle, leaving a loose end 2 cm (¾ in) long held in place with reusable adhesive.

6 Once completed, cut a slit in the loose end with a craft knife and thread the last stitch through this on the underside of the coaster. Pull tightly and tuck behind other stitches to secure. Trim off the remainder.

MATERIALS AND EQUIPMENT YOU WILL NEED

THICK SUEDE OR LEATHER • SCISSORS • PENCIL • METAL RULER • HOLE PUNCH • LEATHER THONGING • REUSABLE ADHESIVE • CRAFT KNIFE

LEATHER CHAIN BELT

POPULAR IN THE 1930S AND REVIVED IN THE 1960S, THESE SIMPLE INTERLINK BELTS ARE ONCE AGAIN IN FASHION, AND CAN BE WORN TIED AROUND THE WAIST OR THE HIPS, WITH LONG OR SHORT SKIRTS, DRESSES OR TROUSERS. THE SHAPE OF THE LINKS CAN BE CHANGED; EXPERIMENT BY CUTTING OUT PATTERNS IN FOLDED PIECES OF PAPER. YOU WILL NEED A LEATHER THAT IS THICK ENOUGH TO HOLD ITS FORM BUT THIN ENOUGH TO FOLD EASILY.

1 Using the template at the back of the book, cut out enough suede or leather shapes to fit around your waist, allowing one shape for each 2.5 cm (1 in). Glue two shapes together and leave to dry. Cut out the centre circles in all of the other shapes.

3 Continue adding links, making sure that you have an even number on both sides of the central shape, until the belt is the correct size.

5 Tie knots in both ends of each shoelace. Apply a little glue to the uncut ends of the fringing and roll up the fringes around the ends of the shoelaces. Secure with thin strips of leather thonging and glue or tie to hold in place.

2 Cut out the circles from the doubled shape and use this as the centre back of the belt. Attach the other sections of the belt by linking them through the holes and doubling them over, as shown.

4 Cut out four strips from the same suede or leather, each measuring 5 x 7 cm (2 x 2¾ in). Fold over each piece lengthways and glue the ends together. When dry, snip a fringe along the folded edge about 1.5 cm (⅝ in) deep.

6 Loop and knot a shoelace through one end of the belt, as shown. Repeat with the second shoelace at the other end of the belt. These will act as ties.

MATERIALS AND EQUIPMENT YOU WILL NEED

SMALL SCISSORS • THIN SUEDE OR LEATHER • PVA (WHITE) GLUE • LONG SHOELACES • RULER • LEATHER THONGING

SHEEPSKIN-BOUND ORGANIZER

A PERSONAL ORGANIZER IS A USEFUL PRESENT FOR ANYONE IN THEIR TEENS AND OLDER. THIS NOTEBOOK IS VERY STYLISH AND THE LAMBSKIN COVER MAKES IT HIGHLY INDIVIDUAL. THE BUNNY ACCESSORY ADDS A WITTY TOUCH TO THE LIPSTICK HOLDER, BUT IT IS AN OPTIONAL DETAIL AND CAN EASILY BE LEFT OFF.

1 Cut out the following elements: 29 x 19.5 cm (11½ x 7¾ in) lambskin cover; 29 x 19.5 cm (11½ x 7¾ in) thin leather lining; two pieces of stiff leather, 18.5 x 10 cm (7¼ x 4 in); 18.5 x 10 cm (7¼ x 4 in) thin leather lining for the pocket wallet; 15 x 4 cm (6 x 1½ in) lambskin strap; and 90 x 10 cm (36 x 4 in) lining fabric.

2 Cut out a rectangle of cardboard to measure 28 x 18.5 cm (11 x 7¼ in). Partially cut two parallel lines 4 cm (1½ in) apart down the centre of the board to make a spine.

3 Reinforce this spine with strips of open-weave bandage. Glue these over the cuts with PVA (white) glue and let dry.

4 Turn over the cardboard and spread an even layer of PVA (white) glue over the back. Then glue the lining into position on the cardboard, smoothing it down with a bone folder. Leave to dry under a heavy weight to prevent warping. Then trim all around the edges.

5 Place the ring binder in position on the inside spine and mark the position of the holes. Punch the holes using a No 6 hole punch. Rivet the ring binder in place.

6 Sew the strap to the lambskin cover midway along the back, using embroidery cotton (floss). Then make a loop big enough to fit a pencil through and secure with backstitch. To add the lipstick holder, stitch a finger puppet on to the strap. Stitch the Velcro tape in place on the inside of the strap and on the front cover, making an allowance for bulk. ▶

MATERIALS AND EQUIPMENT YOU WILL NEED

SCISSORS • 1 LAMBSKIN • THIN LEATHER FOR LINING • THIN STIFF LEATHER FOR WALLETS • LINING FABRIC • CUTTING MAT • CRAFT KNIFE • CARDBOARD • METAL RULER • OPEN-WEAVE BANDAGE • PVA (WHITE) GLUE • BONE FOLDER • 6-RING RING BINDER • HOLE PUNCH • LONG RIVETS • RIVETING HAMMER • BLOCK OF WOOD • EMBROIDERY COTTON (FLOSS) • PENCIL • GLOVERS NEEDLE • FINGER PUPPET • VELCRO TAPE • IRON

7 Using PVA glue, attach the lambskin cover to the outside of the notebook. Weight two books on either side of the spine to prevent warping. Leave to dry.

8 Starting at 4 cm (1½ in) from the end, mark out 5.5 cm (2¼ in) intervals on the long strip of lining fabric. Leave 7.5 cm (3 in) unmarked at the end. Fold the fabric at the marked points and iron accordian-style.

9 On the inside of the front wallet, mark out curved slits for the pockets, lining them up with the folds in the lining fabric. Cut out the curved slits. Shade all but the pocket slits as the gluing area, and run PVA above each slit and around the edge of the inside wallet. Glue beneath the first 4 cm (1½ in) section under the last pocket slit. Then glue along each overlapping fold until you reach the top.

10 Glue the wallet front over the folded pockets and weight down with a heavy book until dry.

11 When the glue is dry, trim around the edges, cutting off and discarding any excess fabric. Iron the wallet flat.

12 Overstitch all around the edge of the cover from inside to outside, while securing the outside edges of the wallet using thick embroidery cotton (floss) and a glovers needle.

SHOPPING BAG

THIS FASHIONABLE BAG, MADE FROM THICK RED SUEDE AND STITCHED TOGETHER WITH ROYAL BLUE SUEDE THONGING, IS EASIER TO MAKE THAN IT LOOKS. THE HANDLES HAVE ROPE CORES WHICH, WHEN WRAPPED IN SUEDE, MAKE A COMFORTABLE GRIP. THE BAG IS DESIGNED TO TAKE A MODERATE AMOUNT OF SHOPPING, SO DON'T FILL UP ON HEAVY CANS AND JARS. THE BRIGHTLY CONTRASTING COLOURS CHOSEN HAVE A CHEERY FEEL AND ARE SURE TO BE NOTICED. LEATHER AND SUEDE THONGING COME IN A WIDE SELECTION OF COLOURS, AS DO THE SKINS, SO FEEL FREE TO MAKE YOUR OWN CHOICE.

 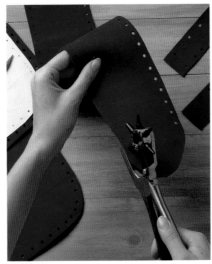 

1 Make a paper pattern following the templates at the back of the book. Using the pattern, cut out two side pieces and one gusset piece from thick suede or leather. Cut two lengths for the straps.

2 Mark holes at regular intervals around the edge of each of the cut-out suede or leather pieces. Punch out the holes using a hole punch.

3 Make the handle attachment holes in each side panel following the instructions explained in Basic Techniques. ▶

MATERIALS AND EQUIPMENT YOU WILL NEED

PAPER • PENCIL • SCISSORS • THICK SUEDE OR LEATHER • HOLE PUNCH (NO 4) • MALLET • BLOCK OF WOOD • ROYAL BLUE SUEDE THONGING • 50 CM (20 IN) ROPE, 2 CM (¾ IN) THICK • PVA (WHITE) GLUE

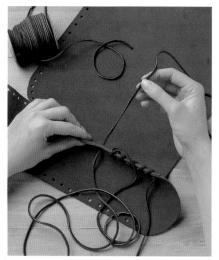

4 Working with a very long piece of thonging and leaving an excess of 15 cm (6 in), lace the thonging through the gusset and one side piece, joining them together.

5 Once one side is complete, start on the other side piece, tying the ends of the thonging together at the top of the gusset.

6 Cut two pieces of rope, each 25 cm (10 in) long. Glue one piece into the centre of each handle and wrap the suede around to encase the rope. Allow to dry.

7 Attach the handles to the side pieces of the bag using 40 cm (16 in) of thonging to make large cross stitches. Start the stitching from the inside top outer corner to make the first diagonal, then make the second diagonal from bottom to top. Secure with a knot on the inside.

8 Punch two holes above the top cross stitch on each handle. Thread through a length of thonging and bind it tightly around the handle to cover it completely.

9 To finish, join both excess ends on each handle with a reef knot to prevent them from unravelling.

KEEPSAKE WALLET

ESIGNED TO KEEP TO HAND AS A REMINDER OF YOUR LOVED ONES, THIS WALLET CONTAINS TWO HEART-SHAPED FRAMES FOR SMALL PHOTOGRAPHS. THE PLASTIC COVERS CAN BE CUT FROM TRANSPARENT PACKAGING, OR FROM ACETATE, AND YOU CAN USE SCRAP PIECES OF LEATHER OR SUEDE TO SAVE MONEY.

1 Cut out the wallet, frames and front patch following the templates at the back of the book. Cut out a heart from the frames and the patch. Cut out a heart for the strap.

2 Cut two pieces of plastic or acetate to fit the frames, and glue them to the wrong side of the frames. Leave to dry, then trim with pinking shears. Cut out a semi-circle midway along the inside edge of both frame pieces. Place a piece of leather behind the heart and glue to the front of the wallet. Glue the cut-out heart on to the end of the strap. Leave to dry.

3 Using the No 1 hole punch, punch evenly spaced holes along all four edges of the front patch. Turn over the wallet. Apply PVA (white) glue along the edges of the inside frames and stick the frames in position. Leave to dry.

4 Punch holes all around the outer edge of the frames, taking care to match up the holes with those on the front. Turn over the wallet. Usng embroidery cotton (floss), stitch a running stitch along the edge of the front patch nearest to the spine; do not stitch through the frames on the inside.

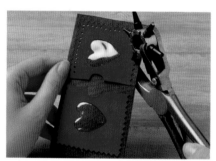

5 Loop a length of thin cord around the spine of the wallet. Add your pictures, then stitch around the outer edge of the wallet, working in and out of the punched holes and securing the cord in place.

6 Cut out a small heart shape from the red Velcro tape. Glue one piece to the heart tab on the fastening strap and glue its counterpart to the centre on the back of the wallet.

MATERIALS AND EQUIPMENT YOU WILL NEED

7 x 18 CM (2¾ x 7 IN) THIN BUT STIFF LEATHER OR SUEDE • SCISSORS • THIN MARKER • CLEAR STIFF PLASTIC OR ACETATE • PVA (WHITE) GLUE
• PINKING SHEARS • SCRAP OF CONTRASTING LEATHER • HOLE PUNCH (NO 1) • THICK EMBROIDERY COTTON (FLOSS) • DARNING NEEDLE
• THIN CORD • SMALL PIECE OF RED VELCRO TAPE

BABY'S BOOTIES

THESE ADORABLE BOOTIES ARE MADE FROM LAMBSKIN, A NATURAL PRODUCT THAT IS WARM AND SNUG WITH THE ADDED BONUS OF BEING WASHABLE. LAMBSKIN IS AVAILABLE IN A SURPRISINGLY WIDE RANGE OF COLOURS, AND ALTHOUGH IT IS STRONG IT CAN BE STITCHED WITH AN ORDINARY NEEDLE. EACH BOOTIE CONSISTS OF JUST TWO PIECES, THE UPPER AND THE SOLE, WHICH ARE SIMPLY STITCHED TOGETHER. ADAPT THE PATTERN TO FIT YOUR BABY'S FEET.

1 Following the templates at the back of the book, cut two soles and two uppers from lambskin. Punch two holes at the marked points on each side of both uppers to make the holes for the laces.

2 Fold the uppers in half with the fleecy side facing inwards and join with a running stitch midway along the front to the tip of the toe.

3 Place the uppers on to the sole and tack (baste) the heel and toe in place. Stitch together using a buttonhole stitch around the edges of the upper and sole.

4 Make a simple overstitch around the holes to create a daisy effect. Thread the laces through the holes to complete.

MATERIALS AND EQUIPMENT YOU WILL NEED

LAMBSKIN • SCISSORS • HOLE PUNCH • NEEDLE • THICK LINEN THREAD • LACES OR THICK EMBROIDERY COTTON (FLOSS)

CHILD'S POMPOM HAT

W HAT CHILD WOULD NOT LOVE THIS DELIGHTFUL WARM HAT WITH ITS PROTECTIVE EAR FLAPS TO KEEP OUT THE COLD WINTER WIND AND ITS PRETTY EMBROIDERED BORDERS? THE HAT WAS MADE TO FIT A YOUNG CHILD BUT YOU CAN ADAPT THE PATTERN TO FIT AN OLDER CHILD OR EVEN YOURSELF: THIS HAT WOULD LOOK JUST AS GOOD ON AN ADULT, ALTHOUGH A MAN MAY PREFER A PLAINER VERSION, WITHOUT THE EMBROIDERED DECORATION.

1 Cut four segments out of lambskin for the top of the hat and one for the brim, using the templates at the back of the book and scaling them up to the required size.

2 Wrap the brim around in a circle. Stitch both ends together with cream embroidery cotton (floss), using a whip stitch.

3 Stitch the quarter segments of the top together in the same way, with the pointed ends at the top.

4 Join the top of the hat to the brim, positioning the two ear flaps on the side segments.

▶

MATERIALS AND EQUIPMENT YOU WILL NEED

1–2 BLUE LAMBSKINS • SCISSORS • 3 SKEINS OF THICK EMBROIDERY COTTON (FLOSS) IN CREAM, BLUE AND MAUVE • GLOVERS NEEDLE •
A BALL OF CREAM WOOL (YARN) • THIN CARDBOARD

5 Stitch all around the edge of the hat brim, including the ear flaps, in blue embroidery cotton (floss).

6 Embroider chain stitch all around the edge of the hat in blue cotton and add a cross stitch (zigzag stitch) decoration in mauve cotton.

7 Cut six lengths of wool (yarn), each about 60 cm (24 in) long. Loop three through the stitched edging on each ear flap tip. Double them over and plait (braid) together. Tie into a knot at the end, leaving a 4 cm (1½ in) tassel. Repeat on the other side.

8 To make the pompom, cut two round pieces of thin cardboard 5 cm (2 in) in diameter, with a 2 cm (¾ in) hole in each centre. Wrap cream wool around the cardboard.

9 Continue wrapping the wool until no more will fit through the central hole. Using sharp pointed scissors, snip through the wool in between the cardboard circles. Separate the cardboard slightly and tightly wrap wool around the middle. Tie to secure, leaving two long ends. Remove the cardboard circles. Trim the wool ends to get an even, round pompom.

10 Thread the two long ends of the pompom onto a glovers needle and stitch through the top point of the hat. Make it really secure, then tie the two ends together and snip off the excess.

LITTLE CHAMOIS DOG

Adelightful stocking filler for a child, this toy comes with button eyes, lead and winter coat. Chamois leather is cheap and accessible: as it is used for cleaning windows, it can be bought in hardware and do-it-yourself stores. It can be stitched with a leather needle and provided that you use a washable stuffing, it can be put in the washing machine. If you are making the dog for a young child under three years old, embroider the eyes rather than using buttons and leave out the accessories, in case the child should swallow them.

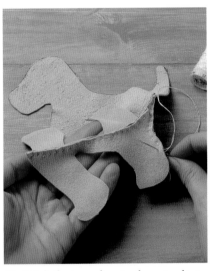

1 Cut out each piece of the dog from chamois leather, following the templates at the back of the book. Place matching pieces together.

2 Using linen thread and a leather needle, stitch together the inner legs along the belly. Use a small running stitch.

3 Stitch the inner legs to the outer legs, making sure that the belly seam is on the outside. ▶

MATERIALS AND EQUIPMENT YOU WILL NEED

PIECE OF CHAMOIS LEATHER • SCISSORS • LINEN THREAD • LEATHER NEEDLE • POLYESTER WADDING (BATTING) • PENCIL • SCRAP OF RED SUEDE • RED LEATHER THONGING • PVA (WHITE) GLUE • SMALL PIECE OF RED VELCRO TAPE • 2 BUTTONS • CONTRASTING EMBROIDERY COTTON (FLOSS)

4 Once the leg sections have been
completed, stitch from the bottom
up around the tail. Stop at the back.

5 Stitch from the front legs along the
neck and underside of the jaw. When
you reach where the mouth would be,
start to sew in the head gusset, one side at
a time. Insert the ears at the top of the
head, as shown.

6 Continue stitching down the back of
the head, then leave the back open.
Stuff the dog, using a pencil to push the
wadding (batting) into the legs and tail,
until it feels firm. Stitch up the back.

7 Cut out all the elements for the coat
and collar from red suede. Cut a
length of red leather thonging for the
lead. Stitch the strap on to the coat, then
glue a small piece of Velcro tape to both
the coat and the strap. Repeat on the
collar. Make a loop at both ends of the
thonging and stitch in place; one loop is
for the hand-hold and the other is for the
collar to thread through. Put the coat and
collar on the dog.

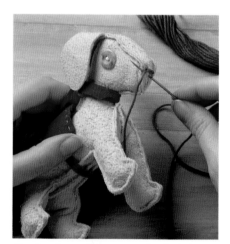

8 Stitch two buttons on the dog's head
for the eyes. If desired, stitch on a
nose, using embroidery cotton (floss).

BLANKET CARRIER

THIS PROJECT SHOWS YOU HOW TO MAKE A BLANKET CARRIER TO USE FOR SUMMER PICNICS AND WALKING EXPEDITIONS, AND IT ALSO SHOWS YOU HOW TO MAKE A BASIC BELT. CHOOSE THE BLANKET PRIOR TO MAKING THE CARRIER, THEN THE MEASUREMENTS CAN BE TAILOR-MADE FOR A SNUG FIT.

1 Cut lengths of belting for the straps, handle, shoulder strap and spacer in an appropriate size for your blanket. Measure and mark 1.5 cm (⅝ in) from the end of each strap. From the centre point of the end, cut to the marking on each side.

3 Holding each strip of leather firmly, bevel all the edges, working on a cutting mat. Try to maintain a smooth, even flow so that the edges are neat and even (see Basic Techniques).

5 Punch 8–10 holes through the straps in an appropriate size for your buckle at intervals of 5 mm (¼ in), starting at 10 cm (4 in) from the pointed end. Punch two pairs of holes on the opposite ends of the straps. These should be 1.5 cm (⅝ in) apart with a 4 cm (1½ in) space between the pairs. Repeat for each belt.

2 Working on the opposite end to the points, shave slivers down the flesh side of the leather for 3 cm (1¼ in) on each belt. Repeat on both ends of the shoulder strap and for 14 cm (5½ in) on each end of the handle strap.

4 Using a damp sponge, moisten the edges of each leather strap in turn. Then vigorously rub the edge slicker along the dampened edges. This will smooth and round the edges.

6 Place each strap in turn on a piece of scrap leather on a block of wood. Position the slot punch midway between the pairs of holes and punch out a slot. Repeat for the second strap. On the shoulder strap, punch four holes at each end of the strap at 5 mm (¼ in), 2 cm (¾ in), 7.5 cm (3 in) and 9.5 cm (3¾ in) from each end. Repeat for the spacer strap. For the handle, punch six holes at 5 mm (¼ in), 2 cm (¾ in), 12 cm (4½ in), 13 cm (5 in), 17 cm (6½ in) and 18.5 cm (7¼ in) from each end. There should be 20 cm (8 in) between the two central holes. ▶

MATERIALS AND EQUIPMENT YOU WILL NEED

FOUR 2 x 110 CM (¾ x 44 IN) COWHIDE STRIPS • LEATHER SCISSORS • METAL RULER • PENCIL • CUTTING MAT • SKIVER • EDGE BEVELLER •
SPONGE • EDGE SLICKER • HOLE PUNCH • SCRAP LEATHER • BLOCK OF WOOD • SLOT CUTTER • PAPER • PROTECTIVE GLOVES •
RIVETING HAMMER • LEATHER STAIN • SATIN SHEEN WAX • CLOTH • PEGS • D-RINGS • RIVETS, LONG AND MEDIUM •
BUCKLES, 2 CM (¾ IN) WIDE • CHAP SNAPS

7 Protect your work surface with paper and wear protective gloves to prevent the leather stain from getting on your hands. Using a damp sponge, stroke the stain over the leather, working in small circles. Ensure that the edges are covered well. Let dry. Apply a second coat later if a darker colour is required. Once dry, stain the underside in the same way.

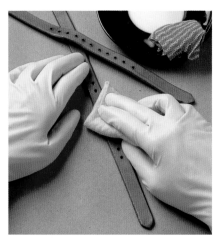

8 Apply a coating of wax over the stained leather with a dry cloth. Buff up the leather to get a sheen.

9 Dampen the handle leather on both sides with a moist sponge. Overlap both ends by 15 cm (6 in) and form two loops at the edges. Peg the loops to hold in place. All three sets of holes should line up on both sides. Mould the shape of the handle with your hands and leave to dry. Slip a D-ring on to each loop. Working on a block of wood to protect your work surface, rivet through the three layers of leather, using medium-length rivets.

10 Fit the centre bar of the buckles behind the punched slots in both straps so that the prong comes through. Using small rivets, hammer into place.

11 Slide two chap snaps on to the shoulder strap ends, making sure the fasteners face inwards. Loop the ends of the shoulder straps to line up the holes and rivet to secure.

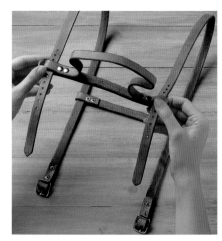

12 Turn over the ends of the spacer strap and rivet to form loops at either end. Thread the straps through these and then through the handle. To complete the carrier, clip on chap snaps for the shoulder straps.

SEWING PURSE

THIS IS A DELIGHTFUL PROJECT FOR AN ADULT OR A CHILD TO MAKE AND IT WOULD ALSO MAKE A WONDERFUL GIFT. ONCE MADE, FURNISH THE PURSE WITH SCISSORS, EMBROIDERY COTTONS (FLOSS), PINS AND NEEDLES. IF YOU ONLY HAVE SCRAPS OF LEATHER, THE PURSE CAN BE MADE IN QUARTERS. MAKE A PATTERN USING THE TEMPLATE AND CUT INTO FOUR ALONG THE FOLDLINES; USE THIS TO CUT OUT THE SHAPES. PUNCH AROUND THE SHAPES AND STITCH TOGETHER.

1 Using a compass, draw a circle measuring 25 cm (10 in) in diameter on each of the following: purple suede for the lining, thick interfacing and red suede for the cover. Cut out the circles.

2 Cut out a 23 cm (9 in) strip of lining suede. Stitch this across the centre of the purple circle, making cross stitches at five points.

3 Cut a strip of purple leather measuring 12 x 2 cm (4½ x ¾ in) to make a strap. Then, following the templates at the back of the book, cut out a leaf and flower from the coloured leather scraps, and a paper pattern for the petal shape of the purse.

4 Place the leaf on one end of the strap and place the flower on top. Punch a hole through both, then rivet them together. Cover the rivet by gluing a round red leather centre over the top. Cut a slot in the red leather circle wide enough to insert the strap and about 2.25 cm (⅞ in) from the edge of the circle. Push the strap in 3 cm (1¼ in) deep and glue this on to the underside. Then glue the interfacing to the underside of the red circle. Leave until the glue is dry.

▶

MATERIALS AND EQUIPMENT YOU WILL NEED

COMPASS • 30 CM (12 IN) SQUARE OF PURPLE SOFT PIG SUEDE, 50 G (2 OZ) WEIGHT • 30 CM (12 IN) SQUARE OF INTERFACING • 30 CM (12 IN) SQUARE OF RED SOFT PIG SUEDE, 50 G (2 OZ) WEIGHT • RULER • PENCIL • SCISSORS • NEEDLE • SEWING COTTON • SCRAPS OF COLOURED THICKER LEATHER • PAPER • HOLE PUNCH • MEDIUM RIVETS • RIVETING HAMMER • BLOCK OF WOOD • PVA (WHITE) GLUE • STITCHING WHEEL • THICK EMBROIDERY COTTON (FLOSS) • EMBROIDERY SCISSORS • DARNING NEEDLE • VELCRO TAPE • FELT

5 Carefully glue the top layer on to the purple layer, sandwiching the interfacing, making sure that the strap lines up with the purple strip. Trace around the petal shape from the pattern, so that the strap is positioned mid-heart. Cut out the shape.

6 Mark 5 mm (¼ in) in from the edge of the petals all around the shape. Mark this out clearly at 5 mm (¼ in) intervals.

7 Using a No 1 hole punch, punch holes all around the edge, following the marked line. Move the strap forwards while you punch behind it.

8 Using contrasting embroidery cotton (floss), stitch the layers together following the punched holes. Glue a piece of red Velcro tape to the inside of the strap, and its counterpart on to the outside of the front in the correct position.

9 Cut out small felt segments and glue to the purple side of the purse with a dab of PVA (white) glue. These are for keeping pins and needles secure.

10 Before folding the actual purse, practise on the paper pattern, checking the picture to see how it is folded. Fold in both sides first, leaving a flat bottom where the inside strip passes by. Then form creases down the sides of the hearts. Use a ruler to achieve a crisp crease. Fold the strap down to close.

PICTURE FRAME

THIS STYLISH FRAME IS MADE FROM TWO THICK PIECES OF LEATHER OR SUEDE, WHICH ARE REINFORCED WITH A SHEET OF PLASTIC, AND GLUED THEN STITCHED TOGETHER. THE BACK SUPPORT IS RIVETED ON TO ALLOW THE FRAME TO BE PACKED FLAT. LIFT UP THE BACK FLAP TO FIT THE GLASS AND PICTURE.

1 Cut three pieces of leather following the templates at the back of the book. Cut the inner rectangle from the front to make the frame. In the back punch two holes at the top corners, and cut the half moon between the two holes.

2 Punch a hole in the base of the back, as marked on the template. Thread cord through, and glue in place. Cut a plastic reinforcer to fit the backing, cutting out a half moon in the position of the backing slit. Cut a support from plastic; glue the backing to the support and to the frame backing. Let dry.

3 Following the templates, punch a hole at the base of the support 1.5 cm (⅝ in) from the edge. Punch a hole in a similar position at the top. Thread the other end of the cord through the base of the support and tie a knot. Punch two holes side by side in both the support and the backing, following the marks on the templates. Rivet the support in place (see Basic Techniques).

4 Punch evenly spaced holes around the edge of the front piece. Glue the backing to the front piece and place under a heavy weight until the glue has dried.

5 Once dry, repunch the holes around the frame, making sure they punch through both the front and the backing.

6 Thread leather thonging in a running stitch around the punched holes, starting from the back bottom corner. Entwine both ends in and out of other stitches at the back of the frame to secure. Add your picture to the frame and fit the glass cover, if using.

MATERIALS AND EQUIPMENT YOU WILL NEED

THICK LEATHER OR SUEDE • LEATHER SCISSORS OR CRAFT KNIFE • HOLE PUNCH • THIN CORD • PVA (WHITE) GLUE • STIFF THIN PLASTIC • MEDIUM LENGTH RIVETS • RIVETING HAMMER • BLOCK OF WOOD • BEIGE LEATHER THONGING • PICTURE • GLASS COVER (OPTIONAL)

WALL POCKETS

THICK SUEDE IN NEUTRAL COLOURS IS USED TO MAKE THIS CHIC WALL OR DOOR HANGING. SUITABLE FOR A FASHIONABLY UNCLUTTERED INTERIOR, THE WALL POCKETS CAN BE USED TO STORE MAGAZINES OR NOTES, AND MAKE THE PERFECT ACCESSORY FOR YOUR HOME OFFICE. DOWELLING RODS ARE THREADE... THROUGH THE TOP AND BOTTOM OF THE HANGING, WHICH IS THEN HUNG FROM HOOKS IN THE WALL. THE POCKETS ARE RIVETED TO MAKE THEM MORE SECURE.

1 Cut out a large rectangle measuring 48 x 110 cm (19 x 44 in) from thick suede. Use a set (T) square to check that the corners are true right angles. Cut out three same-size patches from suede to make the pockets. Arrange them on the background in the desired position.

2 Draw around one of the suede pocket patches on to a piece of cardboard. Use as a guide to mark the stitch holes for the pockets on the backing suede.

3 Punch the holes in the backing suede (see Basic Techniques for how to make holes out of reach of the hole punch). Mark the hole positions on the pockets and punch them out.

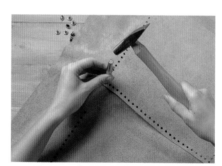

4 Rivet each corner point. Mark out two lines at the top and bottom of the backing suede 7.5 cm (3 in) apart and 1 cm (½ in) from the edge. These will be where the dowelling rods fit later. Punch out a row of holes along each line.

5 Using thonging, sew a running stitch around the edge of each pocket to secure it to the backing. Secure and disguise the ends by threading them through stitches at the back of the hanging.

6 Fold over each end of the backing so that the holes match up. Then stitch these together using thonging. Run a 56 cm (22 in) length of dowelling through each channel. Suspend the wallhanging from hooks in the wall.

MATERIALS AND EQUIPMENT YOU WILL NEED

2.4 M (8 FT) SQUARE OF EGGSHELL BACKING SUEDE, 65 G (2½ OZ) WEIGHT • SCISSORS • LARGE STEEL RULER • SET (T) SQUARE • THREE 30 x 23 CM (12 x 9 IN) PIECES OF SUEDE IN RUST, CAMEL AND CHOCOLATE BROWN, 65 G (2½ OZ) WEIGHT • CARDBOARD 100 x 80 CM (39 x 32 IN) • PENCIL • HOLE PUNCH • SMALL RIVETS • RIVETING HAMMER • LEATHER THONGING • 2 DOWELLING RODS

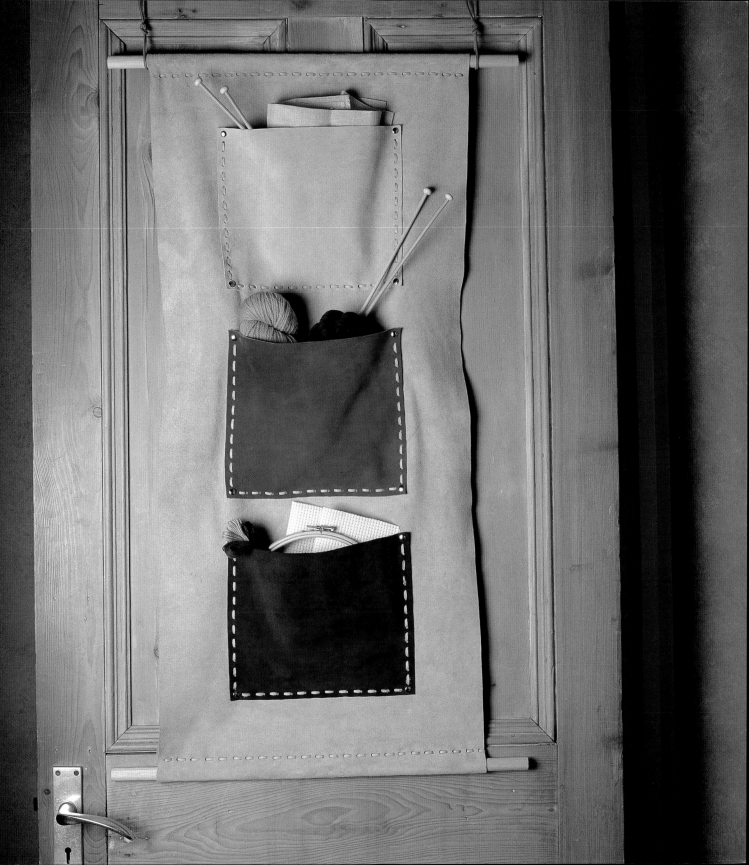

FLORAL HEADBAND AND BROOCH

NATURAL VEGETABLE-TANNED LEATHER IS WONDERFUL FOR MOULDING INTO SIMPLE OR COMPLEX SHAPES. HERE, BY SIMPLY PUSHING AND PINCHING THE LEATHER WITH YOUR FINGERS AND THUMBS YOU CAN MAKE THESE CHARMING ACCESSORIES. CHEERILY COLOURED WITH FELT-TIPPED PENS, THIS IS A SUITABLE PROJECT TO MAKE WITH OR FOR CHILDREN. IF YOU ARE NOT USING WATERPROOF PENS, DAB ON A LAYER OF PROTECTIVE WAX OR FINISH TO PROTECT THE LEATHER.

1 Following the templates at the back of the book, cut out all the elements for the headband and brooch from undyed leather. You may wish to adapt the template design, reducing or increasing the number of flowers to fit your head.

2 Using marker pens, colour in the leather "leaves" on the headband and brooch background.

3 Using thin opaque marker pens, delineate outlines and markings on each flower. Then colour in with thicker translucent fluorescent pens.

4 Dampen all the elements with a moistened sponge, then shape the leaves and flowers with your fingers. Leave until completely dry.

5 Scuff the surface of the leather on the headband and the brooch backing at the points of contact with the flowers. Then glue on the flowers with PVA (white) glue. Attach the brooch backing with strong epoxy glue. Leave to dry.

6 Cut a V-shaped slot in each end of the headband backing. Cut the end of a piece of elastic into a point and slide it through one slot from front to back; glue into position with epoxy glue. Once dry, repeat with the other end, after trying on the headband to check the fitting.

MATERIALS AND EQUIPMENT YOU WILL NEED
SCRAPS OF UNDYED LEATHER • SCISSORS • MARKER PENS • SPONGE • PVA (WHITE) GLUE • LARGE BROOCH BACK • EPOXY GLUE •
ELASTIC, 2 CM (¾ IN) WIDE

HAIR SLIDE (BARRETTE) AND BUTTONS

THE OAK LEAF MOTIF IS AN OLD FAVOURITE, AND IN THESE RICH AUTUMNAL COLOURS IT IS VERY APPEALING. SIMPLE TO MAKE, YOU WILL NEED A TOUGH LEATHER FOR THE BASE LAYER (THE OTHER TWO LAYERS CAN BE THIN) AND A GLOVERS NEEDLE TO STITCH WITH. THE SLIDE (BARRETTE) IS HELD IN PLACE WITH A STAINED BAMBOO KNITTING NEEDLE. THE BUTTONS CAN BE MADE FROM THIN SCRAPS OF LEATHER AND USED TO COMPLEMENT A SEASONAL OUTFIT.

1 Following the templates at the back of the book, cut out two backing ovals and one front piece from different colours of suede or leather. Make the stencil of the oak leaf and draw around it on to the top piece of suede.

2 Cut out the oak leaf shape from the suede using a pair of small scissors.

3 Glue the cut-out top piece on to the first backing piece using PVA (white) glue. Leave to dry.

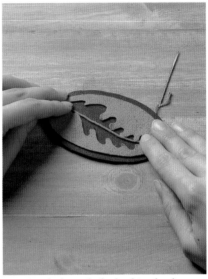

4 Stitch through the backing leather with thick embroidery cotton (floss) to make a central leaf vein. Couch this down with darker sewing cotton (thread). ▶

MATERIALS AND EQUIPMENT YOU WILL NEED
3 PIECES OF SUEDE OR LEATHER • SMALL, SHARP SCISSORS • PEN • PVA (WHITE) GLUE • GLOVERS NEEDLE • SMALL LEATHER NEEDLE •
EMBROIDERY COTTON (FLOSS) • SEWING COTTON (THREAD) • PINKING SHEARS • HOLE PUNCH • SAW • BAMBOO KNITTING NEEDLE • SANDPAPER •
WOODSTAIN OR PERMANENT MARKER PEN (OPTIONAL) • LARGE SELF-COVERING BUTTONS • SCRAPS OF THIN LEATHER AND SUEDE

5 Using embroidery cotton (floss) to match the backing leather, and a glovers needle, make a running stitch border around the edge of the top piece.

6 Trim the backing edge using pinking shears. Then glue on the final backing piece. Once dry, pink the edge of this too.

7 Punch a hole at each side of the oak leaf using a No 6 hole punch. Saw a bamboo knitting needle down to approximately 10 cm (4 in) and rub the end with sandpaper to make a point. If desired, colour the knitting needle with woodstain or indelible pen. Push the knitting needle down through one hole and out through the other to finish the hair slide.

8 To make the buttons, cut out circles of leather or suede large enough to cover self-covering buttons. Cut out one oak leaf shape for each of the buttons from complementary colours of suede.

9 Glue each leaf to a backing circle. Lay a short length of embroidery cotton over the leaf and couch down with darker coloured sewing cotton (thread).

10 Stretch the circle over the button dome, place the backing in position and snap it shut to secure.

TEA COSY

A DD A TOUCH OF THE EXOTIC TO YOUR AFTERNOON TEA PARTIES WITH THIS BEJEWELLED TEA COSY. SIX SECTIONS OF JADE-COLOURED PIG SKIN, LINED WITH FELT AND PADDED WITH WADDING (BATTING), HAVE BEEN DECORATIVELY STITCHED, INCORPORATING A HANDFUL OF GAILY-COLOURED SILK RIBBONS.

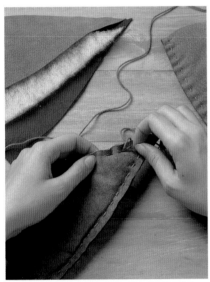

1 Using the templates at the back of the book, cut six segments of cover suede or leather, six segments of felt or non-fraying lining fabric and six segments of polyester wadding (batting). Sandwich one segment of wadding between one segment of suede and one of lining fabric. Hold the layers together by stitching a running stitch all around the sides, using a glovers needle and embroidery cotton (floss). Repeat with the other five segments of wadding, suede and lining fabric.

2 Cut six lengths of silk ribbon to run along the side seams. Stitch together two segments along one side using over-stitch and encasing the ribbon strip along the seam as you go. Add another segment, then stitch three more segments in the same way to make two halves.

3 Fit the two halves around your teapot, and measure the gap in the stitches needed for the handle and spout. Mark these positions. Stitch together the two halves, running two ribbons up each seam so that one will go on each side of the gap.

4 Run a thicker ribbon along the bottom (use a glue stick to keep it in place). Overstitch along the ribbon with a contrasting coloured embroidery cotton at an angle all around the edge. ▶

MATERIALS AND EQUIPMENT YOU WILL NEED
SCISSORS • SUEDE OR LEATHER • FELT OR NON-FRAYING LINING FABRIC • POLYESTER WADDING (BATTING) • GLOVERS NEEDLE •
EMBROIDERY COTTON (FLOSS) • NARROW SILK RIBBON • PENCIL • THICK SILK RIBBON • GLUE STICK • BELL DECORATION •
COLOURED FELT OR LEATHER • PINKING SHEARS • PVA (WHITE) GLUE • FAUX GEMSTONES

5 Using a different coloured thread, stitch the opposite way along the ribbon to create a cross stitch.

7 Cut six large and six small arabesque patches from coloured felt, following the templates at the back of the book. Cut along the bottom edges of the patches using pinking shears.

9 Glue each pair of decorated patches on to the centre of each segment of the tea cosy.

6 Tie all the ribbon ends together at the tip of the cosy, then glue a small bell over the top.

8 Glue a smaller patch on to each larger one. Then glue a faux gemstone to the centre of each.

10 Stitch each patch to secure, using two long stitches on either side of the smaller patch. Alternate the thread colour used on each patch.

COIN PURSE

MADE FROM SOFT AND SUPPLE LEATHER, THIS PURSE HAS A REASSURING AND SATISFYING FEEL, PARTICULARLY WHEN IT IS FULL OF MONEY. IT IS VERY EASY TO MAKE AND ONLY REQUIRES CUTTING, GLUING AND PUNCHING HOLES.

THERE WAS A FASHION IN THE 1940S TO HAVE BAGS SUCH AS THESE LINED WITH FABRIC AND LITTLE POCKETS FOR USE AS SEWING OR MAKE-UP PURSES. IF YOU PREFER, YOU COULD ALSO USE YOUR PURSE FOR EARRINGS AND JEWELLERY PIECES.

1 Make a paper stencil for the purse pieces following the templates at the back of the book. Cut out the leather pieces using the stencil. Mark the positions of the holes using a pencil.

3 Using a No 6 hole punch, carefully punch out the marked holes around the edges of the purse.

5 Repeat with the second shoelace, starting from the opposite side. Pull the strings to make a purse shape.

2 Glue the purse reinforcer on to the main purse piece, with the suede sides facing. Leave to dry.

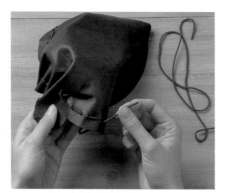

4 Thread both ends of one shoelace from the inside outwards on the lower holes of the reinforcement. Cross over the laces and thread them in and out around each side of the leather circle until they meet at the opposite side.

6 Cut two triangles and two circles from contrasting coloured leather. Punch holes in each shape. Thread the ends of one lace through a circle and a triangle and knot the ends to secure. Repeat with the second lace to complete.

MATERIALS AND EQUIPMENT YOU WILL NEED
PAPER • PENCIL • SCISSORS • 30 X 40 CM (12 X 16 IN) SOFT LEATHER • PVA (WHITE) GLUE • HOLE PUNCH • 2 LONG SHOELACES •
2 SCRAPS OF CONTRASTING LEATHER

CUSHION COVER

SUEDE IS A CLASSIC FABRIC TO USE FOR SOFT FURNISHINGS, AND THESE PASTEL-COLOURED CUSHIONS WOULD LOOK FABULOUS THROWN ON A SOFA.

THE MOTIF USED ON THE CUSHIONS IS OPTIONAL, AND EASILY REPLACED BY ONE OF YOUR CHOICE. TRY IT FIRST USING SCRAP SUEDE TO SEE IF YOU LIKE IT.

1 Make paper templates for the back and front of the cover, allowing a 1.5 cm (⅝ in) seam allowance around the edge. Mark out the templates on the two suede skins, using a tracing wheel. Cut them out.

2 Mark out the motifs for the appliqué from pink suede, following the templates at the back of the book. Cut them out, and cut out a light brown patch of suede on which to stitch the motifs.

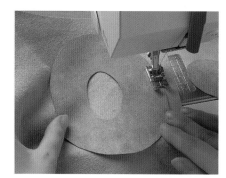

3 Stitch the ellipse shape on to the square patch using a sewing machine fitted with a leather needle and matching cotton. It is best to practise first on scraps of leather to get the right tension.

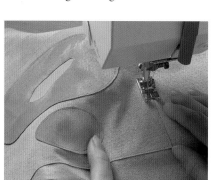

4 Tack (baste) the patch in place on the centre front of the cover piece and stitch on using a sewing machine, in the same way as before.

5 Place both cover pieces together. Position the zip (zipper) and mark its position. Stitch the seam allowance.

6 Place the closed zip in position on the wrong side of the cushion and hold it in place, using a glue stick and tacking (basting) stitches. Turn the right side out and sew the zip into place. Open the zip, turn the wrong side out, and stitch around the remaining sides. Snip the corners and turn the cushion the right side out. Insert a cushion pad and close the zip to complete.

MATERIALS AND EQUIPMENT YOU WILL NEED

PAPER • PENCIL • SCISSORS • 2 SUEDE PIG SKINS • TRACING WHEEL • PINK AND LIGHT BROWN SUEDE FOR APPLIQUÉ • SEWING MACHINE WITH LEATHER NEEDLE • SEWING THREAD • LIGHTWEIGHT NYLON ZIP (ZIPPER) • GLUE STICK • ZIPPER FOOT FOR SEWING MACHINE • CUSHION PAD

OAK LEAF PURSE

ESIGNED TO KEEP YOUR PAPER MONEY AND CREDIT CARDS SAFE, THIS PURSE IS A USEFUL AND ATTRACTIVE ACCESSORY. TAN DEERSKIN WAS USED AS THE BASIC MATERIAL AND IT IS BEAUTIFULLY SOFT AND SUPPLE. THE OAK LEAF MOTIF ADDED TO THE CHOSEN COLOURS OF THIS PURSE HELPS TO GIVE IT AN AUTUMNAL FEELING. BECAUSE ALL THE STITCHING HOLES ARE PUNCHED, THE PURSE IS EASY TO ASSEMBLE WITH A DARNING NEEDLE AND THICK EMBROIDERY COTTON (FLOSS).

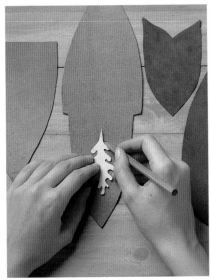

1 Cut out the four component parts from deerskin and soft leather, following the templates at the back of the book. Place the oak template on piece A in the position shown and draw around it with a pencil.

2 Cut out the oak leaf shape using scissors, then glue piece A on to piece B, ensuring that the suede is facing upwards and there is an even border around the edge. Leave to dry.

3 Using embroidery cotton (floss) and a darning needle, stitch through the oak leaf shape from the back and make one long stitch from top to bottom to make a central vein for the leaf. Couch this down with dark brown sewing cotton (thread), using a thin leather needle. ▶

MATERIALS AND EQUIPMENT YOU WILL NEED
21 x 33 CM (8½ x 13 IN) DEERSKIN OR SUEDE • 16 x 22 CM (6¼ x 8½ IN) TAN SOFT LEATHER OR SUEDE • STRONG SCISSORS • PENCIL • PVA (WHITE) GLUE • THICK SAND AND RUST EMBROIDERY COTTON (FLOSS) • DARNING NEEDLE • DARK BROWN SEWING COTTON (THREAD) • THIN LEATHER NEEDLE • PINKING SHEARS • DOUBLE-SIDED TAPE • HOLE PUNCH (No 1) • 1.2 M (4 FT) THIN RUST CORD

4 Trim all around the border using pinking shears.

5 Place piece D on to piece C and tack (baste) together with double-sided tape to hold them in position. Using a hole punch, make holes through both pieces all around the edge of piece D, 5 mm (¼ in) in from the edge. In the same way, punch holes all around the edges of piece A and piece B, as shown. This ensures that the pieces are lined up for stitching.

6 Using contrasting coloured embroidery cotton, stitch piece D on to piece C to form a pocket. Punch holes around the edge of piece C to correspond to piece A. Using rust-coloured embroidery cotton, stitch piece A to piece B around the oak leaf section.

7 Continue stitching with the rust-coloured embroidery cotton to join the pocket section to the backing. Join the two pieces so that the oak leaf section folds over the pocket section.

8 Take a long length of cord and knot the ends together to form a loop with 4 cm (1½ in) ends. Place the knot at the base point of the purse and stitch around the cord to join it to the purse as shown. Once you have reached the top of the front section, stitch back around the purse so that you form a cross stitch.

9 Unravel the ends of the knotted cord to make a decorative tassel.

SHEEPSKIN SLIPPERS

These warm, fleecy slippers are made of soft red lambskin, while the soles are reinforced with thick suede to make them long-lasting and to prevent slipping. The pieces are stitched together with doubled thick linen thread that has been waxed for extra strength and for ease of stitching. The buckles are purely for decoration purposes, but the straps are adjustable and fasten with touch-and-close tape. If the template is too small or large, adapt it to fit by drawing around your own feet.

1 Cut out two pairs of uppers and one pair of soles from lambskins, following the templates at the back of the book.

2 Cut out a second pair of soles, this time from thick leather or suede. Glue the lambskin soles on to the leather ones so that the wool faces upwards and the suede faces down: this will make the soles less slippery when walking. Let dry.

3 Using a stitching wheel, mark a line all around the uppers and soles, approximately 5 mm (¼ in) from the edge.

4 Using double waxed linen thread and a leather needle, stitch up the backs of each pair of uppers. ▶

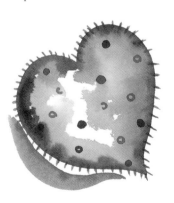

MATERIALS AND EQUIPMENT YOU WILL NEED
2 lambskins • Scissors • Thick leather or suede • PVA (white) glue • Stitching wheel • Ruler • Pencil • Thick linen thread • Leather needle • Beeswax • Velcro tape and matching cotton • Buckles

5 Join the fronts of the slippers together in the same way. Before you reach the ankle, slip your foot into the slipper to find the correct place to stop; this should be approximately 3–4 cm (1¼–1½ in) before the ankle.

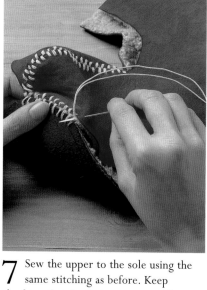

7 Sew the upper to the sole using the same stitching as before. Keep checking that the fitting is correct from toe to heel; you may need to stretch the upper slightly or gather it in a little to fit.

9 Cut a pair of straps from lambskin. Sew around all the edges to prevent stretching. Sew Velcro tape on to one end of the underside of each strap using a matching cotton.

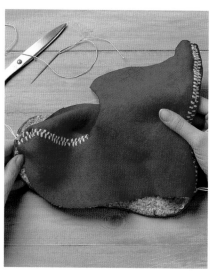

6 Tack (baste) the front and back of each slipper on to its respective sole.

8 Sew down the cuffs on each slipper using a simple running stitch.

10 Attach each strap to a slipper using cross stitches, as shown. Try on the slipper to assess where to stitch the second part of the Velcro tape. Fit the buckles.

LEATHER SATCHEL

THIS CLASSIC PIECE OF LEATHERWORK, FOR USE IN SCHOOL OR OFFICE, IS ONE OF THE MORE INVOLVED PROJECTS IN THE BOOK, BUT IT WILL BE ACHIEVABLE BY THE TIME YOU HAVE WORKED YOUR WAY THROUGH THE SHORTER PROJECTS AND ARE COMFORTABLE WITH THE FULL RANGE OF TECHNIQUES.

1 Make cardboard patterns using the templates at the back of the book. Lay them out on the wrong side of your hide, using the space as economically as possible. Then cut out the pieces and mark the stitching positions around each.

2 Lay the front template on to the front piece of the satchel and mark around the inner edges on the right side of the leather. Bevel the edges of the front pocket, gusset and straps.

3 On the wrong side of the front pocket, mark out hole positions for buckles to be attached later. Punch out the holes.

4 Use the template to mark out the position of the folds in the gusset pieces on the back of the leather. Use a V-groover or a stitching groover to cut into the foldline about one-third of the thickness of the leather. Dampen the cut lines with a moist sponge so that they will cut more easily.

5 Hammer the fold into shape using a leather hammer or hide mallet. The two 45-degree cuts allow the leather to make a 90-degree bend at the corners.

6 Take the pocket gusset and, using a stitching punch and hide mallet, make holes along one edge. Fit the edge against the pocket markings on the front satchel and mark through the holes (this way the holes will line up). Then remake the holes using the stitching chisel. Repeat with the other two sides.

▶

MATERIALS AND EQUIPMENT YOU WILL NEED

CARDBOARD • SCISSORS • SANDLE HIDE • PENCIL • BEVELLER • HOLE PUNCH • V-GROOVER OR STITCHING GROOVER • SPONGE • LEATHER HAMMER OR HIDE MALLET • BLOCK OF WOOD • STITCHING PUNCH • STITCHING CHISEL • STITCHING CLAMP • RIVETS • RIVETING HAMMER • 2 BUCKLES • CLIPS • LINEN THREAD • LEATHER NEEDLE • STITCHING WHEEL • LEATHER THONGING

7 Using a stitching clamp, stitch the front pocket to the gusset. Then rivet the buckles in place (see Basic Techniques). Stitch the pocket on to the front of the satchel.

9 Mark a line around the front, back and spacer. Along the gusset pieces mark the position of holes, then punch these out. It is important that the holes to be thonged line up with each other.

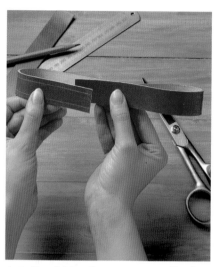

11 For the handle, cut a piece of leather long enough to fit between the straps when looped. Form it into a loop, and line up the overlap positions. Mark holes along the overlap section and punch them out.

8 Punch stitching holes along the edges of the ends of the straps. Place these in position on the back piece of the satchel, and mark through the holes. Punch the marked holes in the back piece. Stitch in place (see Basic Techniques) and neaten with a stitching wheel.

10 Thong the three components together using triple loop (see Basic Techniques) for the centre piece, which is thicker because of the two attached gussets. Double loop for the front and back.

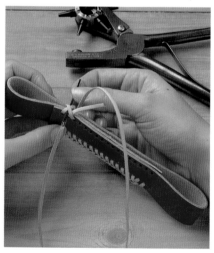

12 Thong the handle together using a triple loop. Lace the straps through the handle into position and close the buckles to complete.

INDIAN-STYLE STOOL

DESIGNER STYLING COUPLED WITH A CUNNING METHOD OF CONSTRUCTION HAVE RESULTED IN THIS FABULOUS PIECE OF FURNITURE, WHICH HARKS BACK TO THE DAYS OF COLONIAL INDIA. THE FOLDING THREE-LEGGED STOOL IS MADE BY JOINING JUNIOR BASEBALL BATS TOGETHER WITH A BOLT. THE THICK LEATHER IN A CONTEMPORARY SHADE OF GREEN HAS BEEN REINFORCED AT ALL THE STRESS POINTS, THEN HAND-STITCHED USING THICK WAXED LINEN THREAD. THE EDGING HAS BEEN PUNCHED AND SNIPPED TO CREATE THE PETAL EFFECT, WHICH, WHEN THE STOOL IS FOLDED UP, FORMS A SIMPLE FLOWER SHAPE.

1 Cut three straining eyes to length and join them together at the centre with a bolt. Lock the bolt by centre-punching between the threads. Drill three holes through the baseball bats; each hole should be slightly lower than the last so as to line up with the straining eyes.

2 Thread the bolts through the holes, assembling the legs in the correct order to keep them in line. Place a washer on either side of the wood on each bat. Centre-punch the ends of the bolts to lock position.

3 Make a pattern in thin card (stock) from the template at the back of the book. Mark out the shape on the leather, working carefully around the petals.

4 Cut out the seat without the corner details. Then, using your petal template as a guide, punch the holes as shown. Next, make a template for the seat reinforcers. Draw a round-nosed triangular shape on thin card which will fit inside the petal of a seat corner. Cut three reinforcers from leather. ▶

MATERIALS AND EQUIPMENT YOU WILL NEED

3 STRAINING EYES • BOLT • CENTRE PUNCH • HAMMER • BLOCK OF WOOD • DRILL • 3 JUNIOR BASEBALL BATS • 6 WASHERS • THIN CARD (STOCK) • PENCIL • LEATHER • LEATHER SCISSORS • CLIPS • HOLE PUNCH • PVA (WHITE) GLUE • CRAFT KNIFE • STITCHING WHEEL • STITCHING CLAMP • LEATHER NEEDLE • LINEN THREAD • SCRAP PIECE OF THICK SUEDE

5 Complete the cutting out of the seat, working carefully around the petal detail using leather scissors.

7 Draw a circular template on card to fit inside the petal. Scratch around it, then use the stitching wheel to mark stitch positions on the right side of the leather.

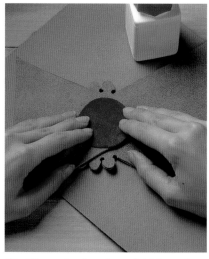

9 Glue a circular piece of thick suede over the stitches on the inside of each corner and leave to dry. This will act as padding to reinforce the stress points.

6 Mark the positions of the reinforcing pieces on each corner. Apply glue sparingly to the flesh sides and stick down the reinforcing pieces. Leave to dry.

8 Fit the area to be sewn into the jaws of a stitching clamp. Then back stitch the marked circle where the stitching wheel has pricked. Repeat for the other two corners.

10 Fold over the reinforcers and mark stitch lines along both side edges of each. Stitch these all in place using back stitch. To lock the stitches, go back over the last couple of stitches as shown and trim off the excess thread. Fit the leather seat over the legs to complete.

CHILD'S WAISTCOAT (VEST)

WITH ITS FOLK ART APPEAL AND ITS WARM PRACTICALITY, THIS WAISTCOAT (VEST) IS THE PERFECT GARMENT FOR YOUR CHILD TO WEAR THIS WINTER. WAISTCOATS PROVIDE PROTECTION AGAINST COLD AROUND THE MOST IMPORTANT AREA, THE CHEST, WHILE ALLOWING THE CHILD FREEDOM OF MOVEMENT, AND WHAT BETTER THERMAL INSULATOR THAN NATURAL WOOL? LAMBSKINS ARE AVAILABLE IN A HUGE NUMBER OF EXCITING COLOURS FROM THE SUPPLIERS LISTED AT THE BACK OF THE BOOK, WHO ONLY SELL SKINS FROM THE NATURAL CASUALTIES OF THE LAMBING SEASON.

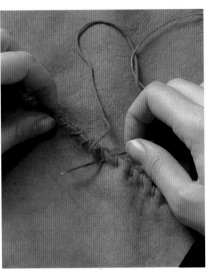

1 Cut out two front pieces, two back pieces and two pockets from one of the lambskins, following the templates at the back of the book.

2 Place the two back pieces side by side, with the woolly sides of the lambskin together, and overstitch the centre back seam using embroidery cotton (floss) and a glovers needle.

3 Overstitch the centre back seam in the opposite direction to make a cross stitch (zigzag stitch) effect. ▶

MATERIALS AND EQUIPMENT YOU WILL NEED
2 LAMBSKINS • SCISSORS • THICK EMBROIDERY COTTON (FLOSS) IN TAN, MAUVE AND BLUE • GLOVERS NEEDLE • RED WOOL (YARN)

4 Stitch the side seams and shoulder seams together and then overstitch as in Step 3.

5 Stitch all around the edge of each armhole to neaten.

6 Stitch along the top edge of each pocket, using red wool (yarn). Embroider chain stitch in mauve around the edge of each pocket and add three blue cross stitches on each as shown.

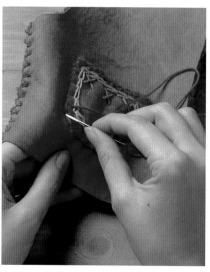

7 Stitch the pockets in position on the front of the waistcoat (vest).

8 Stitch around the unfinished edges of the waistcoat using the same stitch.

9 Decorate the front of the waistcoat with chain stitch and cross stitch, as shown. Cut six 60 cm (24 in) strands of red wool. Loop three through the edge stitching on each front central edge at breastbone position. Double these over, then plait (braid) each side to a suitable length. Tie a knot at the end of each and trim the excess wool to complete the ties.

SUMMER SANDALS

LEATHER SANDALS ARE ESSENTIAL SUMMERWEAR FOR CHILDREN AND ADULTS ALIKE, WHETHER FOR WEEKEND TRIPS TO TOWN, AT HOME OR ON THE BEACH. AS ONE OF THE MORE INVOLVED PROJECTS IN THE BOOK, IT WILL BE HELPFUL TO HAVE MASTERED THE BASIC TECHNIQUES OF CUTTING, PUNCHING AND SEWING LEATHER BEFORE YOU BEGIN. TEMPLATES ARE PROVIDED AT THE BACK OF THE BOOK, BUT YOU MAY WANT TO ADAPT THE SIZES TO FIT YOU OR YOUR FAMILY'S FEET.

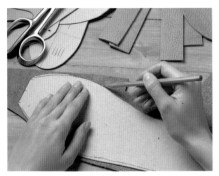

1 Make cardboard templates of all the pattern pieces required, following the templates at the back of the book. Cut out the pieces from leather, using the templates. Adapt the size of the templates by drawing around your own feet.

3 Mark out the hole positions on each sole following the templates. Punch out each of the holes, then cut a slot using a metal ruler and a craft knife. Support the leather on a block of wood to protect your work surface.

5 Assemble the sandal by fitting it around the foot. Allow a 1.5 cm (⅝ in) gap between the laced upper section to allow for stretch in the leather. Mark where the straps and sole meet. Slide the straps through the slots and line up the marked positions.

2 Clip the side uppers pattern to the leather pieces and punch the hole positions in all four uppers as shown. Lace the uppers into pairs.

4 Make strap and lace slots at the points marked on the pieces for the heel and tongue by punching holes at each side and cutting slots.

6 Allowing for a 2.5 cm (1 in) turn under, cut off the excess straps. Scrape the flesh sides of the strap ends. ▶

MATERIALS AND EQUIPMENT YOU WILL NEED

CARDBOARD • PENCIL • SCISSORS • LEATHER • CLIPS • HOLE PUNCH • LACES • METAL RULER • CRAFT KNIFE • BLOCK OF WOOD • SKIVER • PVA (WHITE) GLUE • RIVETS • RIVETING HAMMER • 2 BUCKLES • HIDE MALLET • EYELET KIT • MID-SOLE CUSHIONING • LEATHER FOR TOP SOLE • STRONG GLUE • THICK LINEN THREAD AND NEEDLE (OPTIONAL) • 2 RUBBER SOLES

7 Reassemble the sandal, gluing the strap ends into position on the underside of the sole. Leave to dry. Thread the end of the tongues through each toe slot and glue into position. Leave to dry. Making sure the strap on the heel fits the foot, slide the heel end strap through the sole and glue in place. Let dry.

8 Rivet the strap on to the inside of the sandal (see Basic Techniques) after checking for the best position.

9 Rivet the buckles in place at the outside ankle, as before.

10 Hammer eyelets into position at the lace holes, using a hide mallet and an eyelet kit. Then assemble the heel of the sandal by sliding the strap through the slot at the back of the top heel piece.

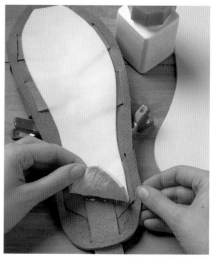

11 Glue the mid-sole cushioning to the underside of the sole, leaving a good selvage all around. Leave to dry.

12 Glue on the top sole so that the cushioning is sandwiched between it and the sandal. Let dry. To strengthen the sandal, you can stitch through the upper connection points. Finally, glue a rubber sole over the top sole and let dry (this can be done by a cobbler, if preferred). Make a second sandal to complete the pair.

TEMPLATES

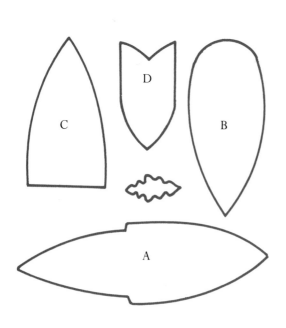

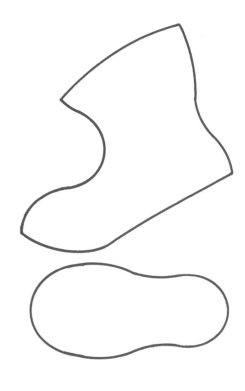

OAK LEAF PURSE PP73–74

BUNNY EGG COSIES PP28–29

SHEEPSKIN SLIPPERS PP75–77

LEATHER CHAIN BELT PP32–33

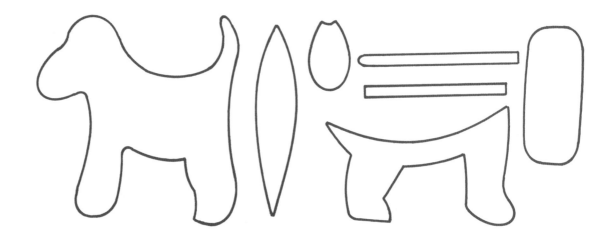

LITTLE CHAMOIS DOG PP47–49

PICTURE FRAME PP56–57

BABY'S BOOTIES PP42–43

SEWING PURSE PP53–55

INDIAN-STYLE STOOL PP81–83

CHILD'S WAISTCOAT (VEST) PP84–86

KEEPSAKE WALLET PP40–41

TEA COSY PP65–67

CHILD'S POMPOM HAT PP44–46

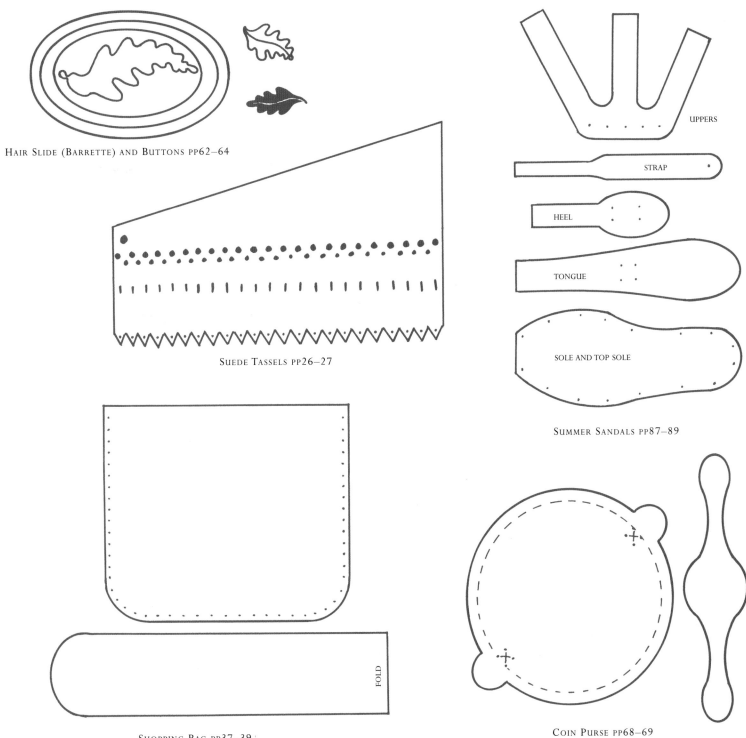

HAIR SLIDE (BARRETTE) AND BUTTONS PP62–64

SUEDE TASSELS PP26–27

SHOPPING BAG PP37–39

FOLD

UPPERS

STRAP

HEEL

TONGUE

SOLE AND TOP SOLE

SUMMER SANDALS PP87–89

COIN PURSE PP68–69

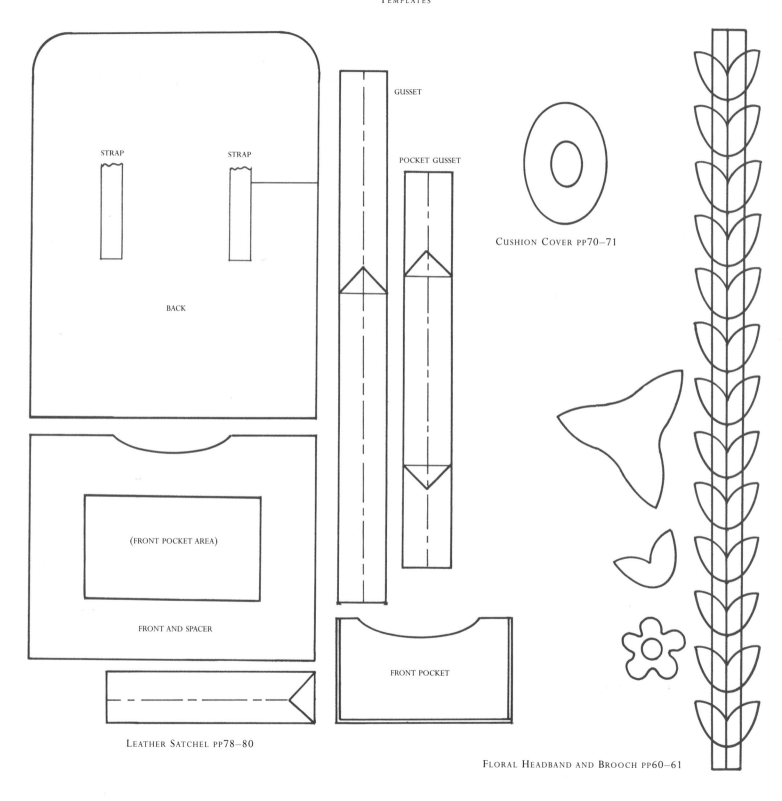

STRAP

STRAP

BACK

GUSSET

POCKET GUSSET

CUSHION COVER PP70–71

(FRONT POCKET AREA)

FRONT AND SPACER

FRONT POCKET

LEATHER SATCHEL PP78–80

FLORAL HEADBAND AND BROOCH PP60–61

SUPPLIERS & ACKNOWLEDGEMENTS

SUPPLIERS

UNITED KINGDOM
Abbey Saddlery
Marlborough Close
Parkgate Industrial Estate
Knutsford WA16 8NF
Tel: (01565) 650 343

Alma Leather Ltd
Unit D
12/14 Great Orex Street
Aldgate
London E1 5NF
Tel: (020) 7375 0343

J.T. Batchelor
9–10 Culford Mews
London N1 4DZ
Tel: (020) 7254 2962

A. & A. Crack
18 Henry Street
Northampton
Tel: (01604) 232 135

Hewit & Son Ltd
Unit 28
Park Royal Metro Centre
Britannia Way
off Coronation Street
London NW10 7PR
Tel: (020) 8965 5377

Pearce Tandy Ltd
Billing Park
Wellingborough Road
Northampton NN3 4BG
Tel: (01604) 407 177

Shepherds Bookbinders Ltd
76 Rochester Row
London SW1P 1JU
Tel: (020) 7630 1184

UNITED STATES
Berman Leathercraft
25LJ Melcher Street
Boston
Massachusetts 02210–1599
Tel: (617) 426 0870

Flannagan Saddlery Hardware
  Corp.
370 Mclean Avenue
Yonkers
New York 10705
Tel: (914) 968 9200

Horween Leather Co.
2015 Elston Avenue
Chicago
Illinois 60614

Tandy Leather Co.
P.O. Box 2934
Fort Worth
Texas 76113

Zack White Leather Co.
1515 Main Street
P.O. Box 315
Ramseur
North Carolina 2736
Tel: (336) 824 4488

For suppliers in Canada, contact
the Canadian Society of Creative
Leathercraft, 1357 Baldwin
Street, Burlington, Ontario.

AUSTRALIA AND NEW ZEALAND
E. Astley & Sons Ltd
44 Portage Road
New Lynn
Auckland
New Zealand
Tel: (Auckland) 875 759

For suppliers in Australia,
contact the Leathercrafters
Guild of South Australia, P.O.
Box 370, Campbelltown 5074.

PICTURE CREDITS

The publishers would like
to thank the following for
permission to reproduce
pictures in this book:
page 8, Christie's Images;
page 9, E. T. Archive (top)
and Christie's Images (bottom);
page 10, Christie's Images;
page 11, Christie's Images.

ACKNOWLEDGEMENTS

The author and publishers would
like to thank the following artists for
supplying the pieces photographed
in this book:
Todd Barber, p15; José Bernardo,
p14; Penny Boylan, pp70–1;
Andrew Gilmore, pp50–2, 78–80,
81–3, 87–89; Garry Greenwood, p13;
Steven Harkin, p13; Rex Lingwood,
p14; Mary Maguire, pp26–7, 28–9,
30–1, 32–3, 34–6, 37–9, 40–1, 42–3,
47–9, 53–5, 56–7, 58–9, 60–1, 62–4,
65–7, 68–9, 72–4, 75–7; Claire
Macauley, pp44–6, 84–6; Tim Meagher,
p15; Jun Nakahama, p15; Peter
Norrington, p12, p14; Valerie Michael,
p14; Stephanie Rothemund, p13;
Paul Seville, p13; Philip Smith, p12.

INDEX